Formerly
New Directions for
Mental Health Services

Editor-in-Chief

# NEW DIRECTIONS FOR YOUTH DEVELOPMENT

*Theory*
*Practice*
*Research*

spring 2003

# When, Where, What, and How Youth Learn

## Blurring School and Community Boundaries

Karen J. Pittman
Nicole Yohalem
Joel Tolman

*issue*
*editors*

JOSSEY-BASS
A Wiley Imprint
www.josseybass.com

WHEN, WHERE, WHAT, AND HOW YOUTH LEARN:
BLURRING SCHOOL AND COMMUNITY BOUNDARIES
*Karen J. Pittman, Nicole Yohalem, Joel Tolman* (eds.)
New Directions for Youth Development, No. 97, Spring 2003
*Gil G. Noam,* Editor-in-Chief

Microfilm copies of issues and articles are available in 16mm and 35mm, as well as microfiche in 105mm, through University Microfilms Inc., 300 North Zeeb Road, Ann Arbor, Michigan 48106-1346.

ISSN 1533-8916 (print)    ISSN 1537-5781 (online)

NEW DIRECTIONS FOR YOUTH DEVELOPMENT is part of The Jossey-Bass Psychology Series and is published quarterly by Wiley Subscription Services, Inc., A Wiley company, at Jossey-Bass, 989 Market Street, San Francisco, California 94103-1741. Periodicals postage paid at San Francisco, California, and at additional mailing offices. Postmaster: Send address changes to New Directions for Youth Development, Jossey-Bass, 989 Market Street, San Francisco, California 94103-1741.

SUBSCRIPTIONS cost $75.00 for individuals and $149.00 for institutions, agencies, and libraries. Prices subject to change. Refer to the order form at the back of this issue.

EDITORIAL CORRESPONDENCE should be sent to the Editor-in-Chief, Dr. Gil G. Noam, Harvard Graduate School of Education, Larsen Hall 601, Appian Way, Cambridge, MA 02138 or McLean Hospital, 115 Mill Street, Belmont, MA 02478.

Cover photograph by PhotoDisc, Inc.

www.josseybass.com

# Contents

# Issue Editors' Notes

LEARNING CROSSES boundaries—time boundaries, place boundaries, and people boundaries. Young people learn lots of things, in lots of ways, and in lots of settings. Policymakers zoom in on academic performance, but parents and young people understand two things very well. First, academic competence, although critical, is not enough to prepare young people for the responsibilities of either adolescence or adulthood. Second, academic competence cannot be nurtured in a vacuum; young people's cognitive development is inextricably linked to a range of other domains, such as social-emotional, psychological, physical, moral, and civic development.

Paul Hill, one of the authors of *It Takes a City*, suggests that "the traditional boundaries between the public school system's responsibilities and those of other community agencies are themselves part of the educational problem."[1] Rather than reform schools, Hill and his colleagues suggest that communities ask a different question: How can our community use all its assets to provide the best education for all of our children?[1]

The answer, wonderfully documented in the eight chapters in this volume, is to blur the lines and connect the dots. Asking teachers and learners where, when, why, and how learning happens almost immediately uncovers the need to see the school day and the school building not as fortresses of learning but anchor points on a learning continuum. Challenging assumptions about who wants to or needs to learn and about what learning is important can level the playing field among providers and move communities a step closer toward Hill's vision.

The first three chapters are broad in scope, challenging conventional notions of when, where, how, and why learning happens. In

NEW DIRECTIONS FOR YOUTH DEVELOPMENT, NO. 97, SPRING 2003 © WILEY PERIODICALS, INC.

Chapter One, Merita Irby, Karen Pittman, and Joel Tolman explore why expanding commitments to learning are critical and present a framework for thinking about broadened definitions of learning. In Chapter Two, Adria Steinberg, Cheryl Almeida, and Lili Allen describe characteristics of effective learning environments for urban adolescents and explore exciting new structures and organizational arrangements that are succeeding in meeting the needs of some of the most vulnerable youth. In Chapter Three, Richard Tagle describes how the Public Education Network is supporting the development of learning-centered communities and the important role that public engagement plays in broadening definitions and linking ideas and institutions.

The next two chapters focus primarily on learning that originates in the community—outside the school day and outside the school building—but the authors also explore the relationship between those learning experiences and the goals and practices of school-based learning. Joan Wynn describes in Chapter Four a framework for transforming the nonschool hours for teenagers and in particular explores the challenges that the After School Matters initiative in Chicago is facing, such as developing strategies for documenting and acknowledging the learning that happens across settings.

In Chapter Five, Lynn Dierking and John Falk discuss the nature and role of free-choice learning—learning that is intrinsically motivated and under the control of the learner—and how it can supplement the outcomes typically associated with schooling. They highlight programs offered by science museums and describe the impact such programs have on youth and families' understanding of science, future aspirations, and attitudes toward learning.

The two chapters that follow focus primarily on school-based learning, but consider how that learning can be enhanced and transformed through intentional connections to community. In Chapter Six, Thomas Del Prete and Laurie Ross describe the challenge of blurring school-community lines in the context of the Worcester, Massachusetts, district-community plan for reinventing high schools. In Chapter Seven, Martin Blank, Sheri DeBoe Johnson, and Bela Shah explore how the community can serve as a valuable resource for learning during not just the nonschool hours but the school day itself. The authors bring to life the community-as-text concept by describing specific approaches and recommendations for moving this idea forward.

In the final chapter, Gil Noam explores the unique potential of after-school programs to support learning that is aligned with no single institution but rather emerges from new collaborative spaces formed by networks of community resources. In doing so, he illustrates varying degrees of bridging that takes place between after-school programs and schools.

The authors whose ideas are collected here share a steadfast belief in at least two principles: that young people are more engaged when they see connections between school-based learning and their community life and that schools are one of a range of learning environments that share responsibility for helping young people learn and develop. We believe that the chapters in this volume offer a collection of innovative ideas and concrete examples that can both inspire and equip practitioners, policymakers, and researchers to act on these principles.

Karen J. Pittman
Nicole Yohalem
Joel Tolman
*Issue Editors*

### Notes

1. Hill, P., Campbell, C., & Harvey, J. (2000). *It takes a city: Getting serious about urban school reform.* Washington, DC: Brookings Institution Press. p. 77.

KAREN J. PITTMAN *is executive director of the Forum for Youth Investment, and president of Impact Strategies, both in Washington, D.C.*

NICOLE YOHALEM *is senior program manager at the Forum for Youth Investment in Washington, D.C.*

JOEL TOLMAN *is senior program associate at the Forum for Youth Investment in Washington, D.C.*

# Executive Summary

*Chapter One: Blurring the lines: Expanding learning opportunities for children and youth*

Merita Irby, Karen J. Pittman, Joel Tolman

It will take communitywide commitments to learning to ensure that young people are problem free, fully prepared, and fully engaged. This chapter articulates a vision where young people have time for deeper, more deliberate learning experiences inside and outside school, during the school day and beyond. The vision involves adding up and maximizing the convergence of four current trends:

- To enrich student learning during the school day, schools are forming partnerships with businesses, universities, artists, health and social service agencies, and nonprofits to bring additional expertise and services into schools and offer off-campus opportunities for learning, work, service, and preventive supports.
- To create additional opportunities for learning, especially for those who have fallen behind, schools are moving beyond commitments to provide extracurricular activities and summer schooling to house, if not provide, formal out-of-school programs for students, particularly those in the elementary grades.
- To build alignment and connections with the other places where students learn, schools are creating stronger partnerships with a broad array of organizations.
- To fulfill their core commitment to support academic achievement, schools are building more connected and aligned learning

NEW DIRECTIONS FOR YOUTH DEVELOPMENT, NO. 97, SPRING 2003 © WILEY PERIODICALS, INC.

experiences within the school day through new forms of account-ability and efforts to integrate curriculum and change instruction.

With community organizations recognizing they are in the learning business and schools realizing they share responsibility for career and life skills, and policymakers pushing this connection, the time is right for alignment.

## Chapter Two: Multiple pathways to adulthood: Expanding the learning options for urban youth

**Adria Steinberg, Cheryl Almeida, Lili Allen**

Learning environments inside and outside school—show promise of creating pathways to postsecondary education, careers, and engaged citizenship for urban young people fifteen to twenty-four years old. In conducting research for From the Margins to the Mainstream, a multiyear Jobs for the Future initiative, the authors studied an array of places where young people gain the support, learn the skills, and obtain the credentials for a smooth transition to adulthood. The learning environments they studied cluster into four categories: reinvented high schools, secondary/postsecondary blends, education/employment blends, and extended learning opportunities.

The authors summarize key features of these institutional arrangements, highlight specific programs that advance vulnerable young people to a postsecondary credential, and explain why it is so important for urban policymakers to make each of these types part of a growing portfolio of effective learning environments. They conclude by suggesting some first steps that policy and practice leaders can take to make more such environments available to young people.

## Chapter Three: Building learning-centered communities through public engagement

**Richard Tagle**

Learning-centered communities work to ensure that all children meet high academic standards, develop a sense of civic duty and community connection, and acquire the capacity for lifelong learning. In this vein, schools and other local institutions work together to align resources, talents, and opportunities with the needs and assets of children, youth, and their families. Learning-centered communities consider the achievement and success of children and youth to be the ultimate outcome of their collaborative work, and the Public Education Network (PEN) defines achievement and success more broadly, encompassing both academic and nonacademic outcomes.

Transforming communities into learning-centered environments requires the sustainability of policy, practices, and resources, and PEN strongly believes this can be done through public engagement. PEN's public engagement framework involves strategies that include advocacy, strategic planning, and community organizing to engage three distinct audiences: policymakers, stakeholders, and the community at large.

Public engagement has both benefits and challenges. As experienced by local education funds (LEFs) working within PEN's Schools and Community Initiative, the benefits include the identification and prioritization of pressing issues, maximizing existing resources, timely response from policymakers, and the emergence of new leaders. The challenges include the creation of common language, turf wars, and the public notion of traditional roles schools and other institutions play. LEFs are able to address these challenges by highlighting their roles as intermediaries and acting as broker between schools and communities to create supportive learning environments for children and youth.

## Chapter Four: High school after school: Creating pathways to the future for adolescents

Joan R. Wynn

A groundswell of attention is being devoted to the out-of-school hours, but little of this attention is focused on the use of out-of-school time for teenagers. This chapter proposes a strategy for the use of out-of-school time for adolescents, illustrates this strategy in action in Chicago, and discusses challenges it faces.

This strategy involves developing a system of graduated opportunities for adolescent involvement, learning, and contribution in the nonschool hours, including opportunities for participation in engaging activities, apprenticeships with skilled professionals, work site internships, and part-time and summer jobs. Together, these opportunities build on and acknowledge learning that occurs both in and out of school. Beyond creating adequate opportunities, getting them to function as a system requires creating ways for youth to know about and connect with opportunities of interest to them.

Through After School Matters, a major public-private partnership, Chicago is integrating and extending existing programs and resources provided by public institutions, community-based organizations, and the business sector to develop a system of pathway opportunities for young people between the ages of fourteen and twenty-one.

After describing work underway in Chicago, the chapter focuses on two challenges facing a system of this kind: acknowledging the learning and skill building that youth develop in the out-of-school hours and crediting or compensating them for their growing skills and contributions. These challenges are integrally related to reinforcing the learning that occurs in out-of-school settings and are critical to the financing and civic attention needed to generate and sustain a system meant to complement and reinforce learning in and out of school.

---

*Chapter Five: Optimizing out-of-school time:*
*The role of free-choice learning*

Lynn D. Dierking, John H. Falk

Free-choice learning, a new paradigm for the learning that youth and their families engage in outside school, can play an important role in the healthy development of youth, families, and communities. Free-choice learning, which people engage in throughout their lives to find out more about what is useful, compelling, or just plain interesting to them, is guided by learners' needs and interests.

Youth and their families are spending increasing amounts of time engaged in such learning—at home, after work, and on weekends. Consequently, it is an untapped resource that represents a significant percentage of all academic and nonacademic learning in the United States. Through free-choice learning, youth can acquire and develop an understanding of a wide array of subjects, learn basic life skills such as how to collaborate on projects and communicate with others, and develop a sense of leadership and responsibility. Free-choice learning can also yield significant learning in cognitive areas normally considered exclusively school subjects, such as science.

Two studies documenting these findings are presented. The authors argue that a vibrant free-choice learning sector is as fundamental to youth development as are quality schools, a thriving economy, and healthy, safe communities. Each of the three components—formal schooling, the workplace and free-choice learning sectors—needs to be engaged and working together toward common goals. Currently, all three are functioning largely in isolation, each driven by widely differing perceptions of what their goals and role in society should be.

---

## Chapter Six: Blurring boundaries: The promise and challenge of a district-community action plan for systemic high school change in Worcester, Massachusetts

**Thomas Del Prete, Laurie Ross**

This chapter examines the Worcester Education Partnership (WEP) in Worcester, Massachusetts, which is funded by the Carnegie Corporation of New York's Schools for a New Society Initiative. It outlines the five core components of the district-community plan for reinventing high schools, briefly summarizes the planning process that led to their development, and discusses aspects of the collaborative effort that illustrate how bottom-line issues such as resource development, public engagement, accountability, leadership, and vision are being addressed. It pays particular attention to some of the tensions inherent in blurring school-community boundaries to achieve systemic high school change.

The WEP planning process was oriented in part by an emphasis on reenvisioning school-community relationships that support student achievement and youth development. The goal was to foster a seamless environment for growth, encompassing both in-school and out-of-school experiences. Among the most important goals of the planned actions was to see an increase in the achievement of minority and low-income students across the district.

It has proven challenging to reculture schools and communities as more collaborative entities with academic achievement and youth development as their guiding mission. Issues of trust and communication have challenged this process. Yet for all of this complexity, the experience in Worcester indicates that it is possible to cultivate a communitywide educational system that supports the development and achievement of all students.

---

### Chapter Seven: Community as text: Using the community as a resource for learning in community schools

Martin J. Blank, Sheri DeBoe Johnson, Bela P. Shah

The community-as-text approach to learning engages and motivates students by using the resources, challenges, assets, and history of the community as part of the core curricula. Students show greater interest and academic success when content is meaningful and relevant and when it contributes to their sense of community connectedness and pride. When the community is used as text for instruction, young people can become assets in their community, helping to solve specific problems alongside peers and adults.

The authors discuss four different community-as-text models: service-learning, academically based community service, using the environment as an integrating context for learning, and place-based education. Although there are several community-as-text models, the authors suggest that they share common characteristics: a focus on real family and community conditions and challenges; reinforcement and extension of standards-based reform; student engagement and motivation; student involvement in program development, implementation, and evaluation; considering young people as resources to their communities; and collaboration between schools and organizations and individuals in the community.

The authors provide examples of how these strategies successfully play out in school settings. Using the community as text is an important distinguishing element of community schools that work to improve student learning and create stronger schools and healthier families and communities.

## Chapter Eight: Learning with excitement: Bridging school and after-school worlds and project-based learning

### Gil G. Noam

This chapter describes methods for bridging school and after-school programs, using a bridging typology to capture the range of ways in which these connections occur. Bridging types vary in intensity, from after-school programs that are entirely separate from schools (and vice versa) to joint school/after-school models. The chapter also addresses some of the implications for project-based learning for each bridging type.

The bridging typology describes the great diversity in the means and ends of bridging between after-school programs and schools. Programs typically bridge within three domains: Interpersonal, Curricular, and Systemic. These domains are often co-occurring. The most common domain found was Interpersonal bridging, including formal and informal meetings and communication between school and after-school staff. The productivity of these relationships was dependent on whether they were reciprocal or one-way.

The second domain, Curricular bridging, consists of attempted alignments between school and after-school curricula. The positive impact of this bridging depends on clear articulation of goals and consistent development of curricula that engage and challenge children. Systemic bridging is the third domain. It includes shared governance, funding, transportation, and other systems by both schools and after-schools.

The use of relevant project-based learning techniques in after-school programs can reinforce the skills imparted during the school day and enhance children's excitement about academic learning, increasing their motivation to learn. Because after-school projects are labor intensive and time-consuming, making connections to the learning of the school day and being able to access resources from the school day can be a productive model. In addition, the tone of after-school must not be a creative extension of learning rather than a continuation of the school day. The project-based approach allows learning to be more hands-on, more participatory, and more community focused. Thoughtful alignments between schools and after-schools can achieve the deepening of classroom learning while maintaining after-schools as a more informal environment for exploration.

*This chapter explores why expanding commitments to learning is critical and presents a framework for broadening definitions of learning.*

# 1

# Blurring the lines: Expanding learning opportunities for children and youth

*Merita Irby, Karen J. Pittman, Joel Tolman*

The Community Partnerships strategy is based on a radical approach to improving educational opportunities in a city. It acknowledges that the traditional boundaries between the public school system's responsibilities and those of other community agencies are themselves part of the educational problem. . . . The strategy opens new options for education, asking "How can this community use all its assets to provide the best education for all our children?"

Paul Hill, Christine Campbell, and James Harvey,
*It Takes a City*

PAUL HILL AND his colleagues have studied successful school reform efforts in numerous cities. Their conclusion, and the title of their book, is that it takes a city to educate children. Their boldest proposal for reforming K-12 education is to create community partnerships that tap into and organize the full array of educational resources available in communities: in libraries, museums, faith-based institutions, community organizations, and nonprofits. Beyond their responsibility for contracting for publicly funded

NEW DIRECTIONS FOR YOUTH DEVELOPMENT, NO. 97, SPRING 2003 © WILEY PERIODICALS, INC.

schools, these partnerships would "encourage nonschool educational resources" to enrich the school day curricula, leverage public and private dollars for community-based organizations in order to "preserve a portfolio of educational alternatives for the disadvantaged," and "broker health and social service resources to meet children's needs."[1]

Hill, Campbell, and Harvey are ahead of many others in proposing that boards of education be replaced by new community partnerships charged not with maintaining schools but with promoting communitywide supports for learning. But they are anything but alone in their conclusion that what exists for young people outside the school building matters hugely. Nor are they alone in arguing it will take communitywide commitments to ensure that young people are problem free, fully prepared, and fully engaged. Leading school reformers like John Goodlad have been making similar arguments for more than two decades:

The school is not and cannot be . . . the exclusive provider in a community's educational system. . . . The school may be the only institution charged exclusively with the educational function, but the ability and responsibility of others to educate is recognized and cultivated. There is not one agency, but an ecology of institutions educating—school, home, places of worship, television, press, museums, libraries, businesses, factories, and more.[2]

More than ever before, schools and districts seem ready to act on these proposals. Chapter Six in this volume shares the work of one such district (Worcester, Massachusetts). Tom Del Prete, director of the reform initiative, says, "I think it's a real challenge for cities to get to the point where they can claim a coordinated effort in support kids' out of school and in school learning. That's the goal that people should try to reach, but it's not easy. That takes infrastructure and also a common framework."[3]

Perhaps most important, young people themselves are looking for ways to weave together learning experiences in and out of school, as Delonte Briggs, a high school senior in Washington, D.C., says:

My school is called School Without Walls. A big part of our school's phi-losophy is that we use the community as a classroom, which means we have a partnership with George Washington University [GW]. At our school, we have maybe 20 classrooms. We have no auditorium. We have no gym. We have no lockers. We have no playing field. . . . We use all of GW's, and it makes our students much more resourceful. . . . We use a lot of museums. . . . I think it makes people in our school a lot more inde-pendent and focused. And, with a block schedule, we have more time to go to museums, to sit down and listen to all the audio-visuals inside the museums. . . .

I think the reason why I like the schedule is because our school is humanities-based. We always have a connection back to reality, back to life, back to the other disciplines inside the school. That makes a big dif-ference. If you don't have something tying it all together, it just seems like you're going to eight different teachers, learning eight different lessons. . . .

At other schools there seems to be a lot of competition between the after-school program and the school near the end of the school day when programs want the students to go out in the community and do other things. That partnership at my school is a lot stronger than at other schools. Instead of the after-school program fighting to get students let out 15 minutes early so that they can be at their internship on time, there's give-and-take between community partners and the school.[4]

We quote this passage at such length because Delonte Briggs's words contain all the critical elements of the vision we are putting forth. Schools have always had functional partnerships with non-profit organizations, businesses, and agencies that can supplement school personnel and resources and take advantage of school facil-ities. But what this young man describes is far more expansive than what is in place in most schools. Community resources have become a critical part of learning during the school day. In-school learning experiences push the boundaries of the school day, so that young people have time for deeper, more deliberate experiences. School-based learning is connected with learning that takes place in the community; there is a give and take between the two. In the process, learning inside the school day and school building is trans-formed. Let us look at the parts of this vision one at a time (see Figure 1.1):

## Figure 1.1.  Blurring the lines

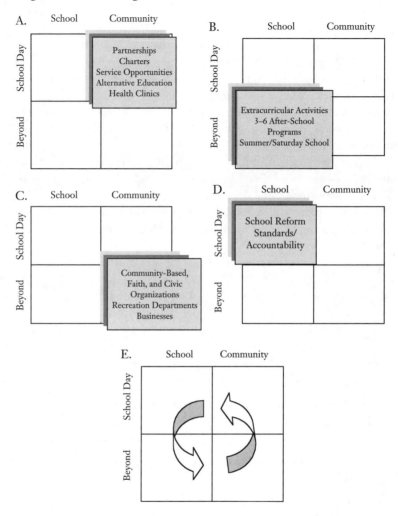

- *To enrich student learning during the school day,* schools are form-ing partnerships with businesses, universities, artists, health and social service agencies, and nonprofits to bring additional expertise and services into the school and offer off-campus opportunities for learning, work, service, and preventive supports (see Figure 1.1A). In some cases, these partners are delegated responsibility for academic education through charters or assume responsibility for educating students who have dropped out.

• *To create additional opportunities for learning, especially for those who have fallen behind,* schools are moving beyond commitments to provide extracurricular activities and summer schooling to house, if not provide, formal out-of-school programs for students, particularly those in the elementary grades (see Figure 1.1B). This trend builds on educators' desires to address students' remedial needs as well as respond to parents' needs for after-school care. There is no doubt, however, that it has also been motivated by federal dollars through the 21st Century Community Learning Centers program, which has provided support for after-school programs (primarily in elementary schools) in over sixty-eight hundred urban and rural schools.

• *To build alignment and connections with the other places where students learn,* schools are creating stronger partnerships with a broad array of organizations: youth-serving organizations, civic and human services nonprofits, faith-based organizations, recreation departments, libraries, museums, businesses, and others, supported by public and private dollars (see Figure 1.1C). These organizations complement schools' focus on academic competence by providing opportunities for civic, social, physical, vocational, and spiritual learning and engagement. Increasingly, they are not only sharing space with schools, but receiving referrals and creating joint ventures such as community schools.

• *To fulfill their core commitment to support academic achievement better,* schools are building more connected and aligned learning experiences within the school day through new forms of accountability, as well as efforts to integrate curriculum and change instruction (see Figure 1.1D). In many ways, the standards movement has narrowed how schools think about learning, but it has also encouraged a new openness. Schools recognize that more time and resources are necessary to meet higher standards and that they will need the help of families and communities to do their job. They also recognize that creating environments in which young people feel safe, known, and respected is a precondition to learning.

Each of these connections is important. The most critical element of the vision, however, is to connect these pieces into something coherent (see Figure 1.1E). This connection is critical so that individual young people understand disparate learning experiences as part of a larger whole. It is equally critical at the community level, where shared accountability for outcomes, consistent community-wide engagement and commitment, compatible definitions of effective learning environments, and ongoing ways to ensure alignment and connection are the critical issues. The challenges in building community connections are enormous, to say the least. Why bother?

## Why expanding commitments is critical

There is broad agreement that all young people need to be fully prepared workers, citizens, parents, and partners. Moreover, public opinion and developmental research agree that academic competence, although important, is not enough. Critical outcomes push beyond academics to encompass moral, physical, civic, social, and vocational goals. Young people need to be problem free, fully prepared, and fully engaged across this range of areas.

If all young people are to be problem free, fully prepared, and fully engaged, we need more time, more people, and more places. Schools do not have the capacity to ensure that all young people are prepared for careers, citizenship, and family and community life. Schools fill at best a quarter of young people's waking hours. And schools have primary responsibility for academic learning, not for the range of areas in which young people need to be learning and engaged.

Schools are only one of a range of learning environments that share responsibility for helping students learn and achieve mastery. Community-based organizations, museums, libraries, parks, workplaces, health centers, and families are not simply places to keep young people safe when they are not in school. Nor are they simply providers of basic services that ensure young people are ready to learn. They are also themselves settings for learning and engagement, appropriately focusing on issues connected to but beyond academic success.

Across settings, there is agreement about what it takes to ensure that young people are fully prepared and engaged. Education and youth development research confirms that effective learning environments provide certain key inputs: stable places, basic services, positive relationships, high expectations, high-quality instruction, and challenging roles. Through its synthesis of research on schools, community organizations, and families, the recent report from the National Research Council, *Community Programs to Promote Youth Development,* lends new credibility to this list by reaffirming the basic features of positive developmental settings:[5]

- Physical and psychological safety
- Appropriate structure
- Supportive relationships
- Opportunities to belong
- Positive social norms
- Support for efficacy and mattering
- Opportunities for skill building
- Integration of family, school and community efforts

Although the characteristics of effective learning environments are similar across settings, learning experiences outside the school day and school building offer an important complement to school-based experiences. Research suggests that students are most likely to be engaged cognitively and emotionally in learning environments outside school.[6] Research on free-choice learning by Dierking and Falk (see Chapter Five, this volume) affirms that the learning going on inside museums, cultural institutions, and other informal settings looks very different from learning inside schools. This research makes clear that nonschool environments are powerful settings for teaching skills and knowledge, using practices distinct from those employed by schools.

Despite the current lack of connection and continuity, the groundwork is in place for much greater levels of alignment and shared accountability. Learning experiences in and out of school are anything but blended. But with community organizations recognizing that they are in the learning business, schools realizing they share responsibility for career and life skills, and policymakers pushing this connection, the time is right for alignment.

## Securing the commitment

The time is right to create strong public-private partnerships and to leverage a sustained commitment to communitywide learning that is as unwavering as the country's current commitment to traditional K-12 education and is linked to public education through a bold new definition of learning. Nothing less than this will afford communities the mandate and resources to weave a web of learning opportunities that can withstand the inevitable fiscal and political pressures that threaten sustained support and growth and create the professional and organizational supports necessary to ensure their continued quality.

The hours between 9:00 A.M. and 3:00 P.M. are the focal point of this country's public commitment to learning. Every child is entitled to a K-12 public education that prepares him or her for postsecondary education, work, and citizenship. Annually, states and localities spend an average of $6,600 per student on public education, which covers six to seven hours per day, 180 days per year. The question will never again be whether to invest in public schools but how best to target that investment.

School reform efforts, including major public and private initiatives focused on the nation's largest and traditionally lowest-performing school districts, have made some progress. But these efforts have fallen short and will continue to do so until they are matched by equally robust commitments to learning in the surrounding community. Communities and schools need to demonstrate a strong and integrated commitment to do the following (see Figure 1.2):

**Figure 1.2.  Expanding commitments**

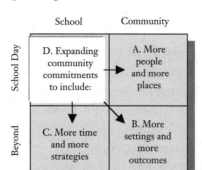

*Forge formal learning links between schools and communities,* bringing
more community learning resources into school and linking students to more places—for example, universities for advanced
courses; museums for hands-on learning; businesses for career
education and structured work experiences; nonprofits for arts,
service, and alternative educational opportunities (see quadrant
A, Figure 1.2)

*Strengthen and expand the capacity of public and private organizations
in the community* that offer civic, social, vocational, and health-
related supports and opportunities, primarily in the out-of-
school hours (see quadrant B, Figure 1.2)

*Expand school-linked out-of-school opportunities,* including traditional
extracurricular activities, but also explore options for increasing
more formal programs, creating community schools that operate after 3:00 P.M., on weekends, and during summers (see quadrant C, Figure 1.2)

*Continue to strengthen traditional classroom instruction,* addressing
issues such as curriculum, professional development, and
resource allocation (see quadrant D, Figure 1.2)

Everything that we know about learning and development suggests two things about the vision of expanded learning commitments illustrated in Figure 1.2:

- No one quadrant can compensate fully for inadequate learning opportunities in another, especially if the weak quadrant is school.
- Other things being equal, more opportunities in more quadrants yield better outcomes.

And everything we know about equity and access suggests that young people with weak learning opportunities in school often have weak learning opportunities out of school.

These realities combine to suggest that we have to be equally intentional about creating learning opportunities in schools and in communities, during the school day and in the afternoon, weekend and summer hours, and that we do this in a way that blurs rather than solidifies the dividing lines that now exist because of funding and accountability decisions.

The good news is that the lines are beginning to blur.[7] Nationally and in individual communities, there is increasing certainty among key education reform leaders that completing the job of reforming schools hinges on the rapid buildup of community-based learning systems. But there is still much work to be done.

## Understanding the challenges

There is nothing easy about the task of building communitywide commitments to learning. The challenges on the school side of the equation are familiar. They are the persistent challenges of school reform: changing long-standing systems of accountability, building constituencies for change, and aligning state and federal policies with local school change efforts.

Whereas the challenges for schools relate to meaningful reform, the challenges for out-of-school and community-based learning are creating "form" in the first place. Two years of work with four cities around the country have convinced us that a common set of tasks faces communities committed to expanding out-of-school opportunities for young people (see Figure 1.3).[8] At the most basic level,

# Figure 1.3. Expanding opportunities: Critical tasks for communities

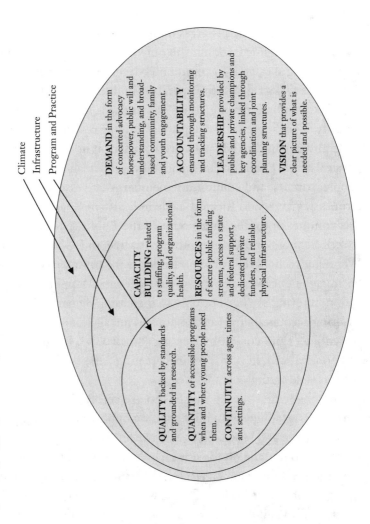

Climate

Infrastructure

Program and Practice

**QUALITY** backed by standards and grounded in research.

**QUANTITY** of accessible programs when and where young people need them.

**CONTINUITY** across ages, times and settings.

**CAPACITY BUILDING** related to staffing, program quality, and organizational health.

**RESOURCES** in the form of secure public funding streams, access to state and federal support, dedicated private funders, and reliable physical infrastructure.

**DEMAND** in the form of concerted advocacy horsepower, public will and understanding, and broad-based community, family and youth engagement.

**ACCOUNTABILITY** ensured through monitoring and tracking structures.

**LEADERSHIP** provided by public and private champions and key agencies, linked through coordination and joint planning structures.

**VISION** that provides a clear picture of what is needed and possible.

quality, quantity, and K-12 continuity are pressing challenges. No city has yet addressed issues of access and equity in a satisfactory manner. Most cities are just now facing issues of quality standards, assessment, and capacity building. And there is not yet a system to lend coherence to the enormous range of community-based opportunities—the challenge of K-12 continuity.

If cities are to make progress on quality, quantity, and continuity, the bottom-line issues in the out-of-school hours, they must face challenges related to community-level infrastructure as well. They face tasks related to capacity—building a capable, stable workforce and addressing issues of standards and organizational capacity. They must build adequate and stable resources to support programs, including adequate transportation infrastructure and physical space. Public engagement and vocal demand—from young people, parents, and community members—are essential to long-term sustainability, as Richard Tagle indicates in Chapter Three in this volume. Both Tagle's account of the Public Education Network's Schools and Community Initiative and Chapter Six on Worcester's school reform efforts indicate the central role that public engagement must play in systems change. Mapping, tracking, and monitoring are key not only to increasing demand but also to ensuring accountability. Leadership and linkages among a range of stakeholders and constituencies are equally vital. Building public and political will, in turn, requires creating and sustaining a vision of what is desired.

The challenges facing those who are reforming schools and those transforming community learning opportunities differ enormously in size and scope. So too do the financial, policy, and institutional resources involved with each. Nevertheless, the challenges center around the same issues: redefining and improving practice, strengthening the capacity of those who teach and lead, and creating structures and policies that support rather than thwart student learning and ground-level leadership.

This common set of challenges, shared by school reformers and those committed to building community-based learning opportunities, help to answer the most basic questions of communities attempting to blur the lines: Should the systems work together? Absolutely. The language is different, but the changes in practices being discussed in school reform parallel the practices that are being encouraged and codified in the out-of-school learning arena. Practices such as team teaching, project-based learning, student advisories, and block classes all have counterparts in the more informal learning environments created by alternative schools, youth organizations, museums, recreation centers, and faith institutions. Resource and requirement levels are different, but both systems are struggling to make professional development more relevant, create better supervision and peer support, link performance to pay, and revamp (or create) preservice credentialing. And at the leadership levels, it is difficult to imagine how changes will be sustained if policies are not agreed to and institutionalized across systems.

Can the systems work together? With difficulty. Sharing space would seem to be a straightforward process, yet even this task raises legitimate concerns about liability, facilities overuse, and shared costs. A logical and important place for the systems to join forces is around training and staffing. Yet this will be one of the most contentious issues to tackle. Teachers and youth workers have different pay scales, benefits, contracts, and bargaining power. Even in cities without strong teachers' unions, debates over who provides the programming can cripple expansion efforts because of the differential cost of hiring tenured teachers compared to part-time youth workers. At the leadership level, principals and program directors have to deal with the fact that the principal has the lion's share of power. This is exacerbated at the district level, where the superintendent does not have a counterpart except in the handful of cities that have created a fully authorized, fully accountable department to handle all public dollars related to community programming for children and youth.

Have these systems worked together in the past? Yes. Leadership came together around the Beacons Schools in New York City in 1991, creating a network that has grown to eighty school-based community centers, run in partnership with community organizations. The mayor and the superintendent in Boston have worked to create literacy programs that blur the school-community lines. Several of the districts participating in the Carnegie Corporation's Schools for a New Society Initiative have ambitious plans for linking school and community learning opportunities.

In the end, reforming schools and forming community-based learning systems are too closely tied to be untangled from one another. Just as important, the critical tasks involved in improving each of these systems are the same: improving practice, strengthening infrastructure, and creating a broader climate conducive to change. If and when schools and communities take on these tasks together—when they blur the lines between these two learning systems—young people's learning experiences will inevitably improve.

## Notes

1. Hill, P., Campbell, C., & Harvey, J. (2000). *It takes a city: Getting serious about urban school reform.* Washington, DC: Brookings Institution Press. Pp. 76–79.

2. Goodlad, J. (1984). *A place called school: Prospects for the future.* New York: McGraw-Hill. P. 350.

3. Interview with T. Del Prete, director of the Worcester Schools for a New Society High School Reform Initiative, Dec. 2001.

4. Tolman, J. (Ed.). (2000). *Learning for life: Youth voices for educational change.* Washington, DC: Forum for Youth Investment.

5. National Research Council and Institute of Medicine. (2001). *Community programs to promote youth development* ( J. Eccles & J. A. Gootman, Eds.). Washington, DC: National Academy Press.

6. Larson, R. (2000). Toward a psychology of positive youth development. *American Psychologist, 55,* 170–183.

7. One city that has tried to increase student outcomes by breaking down some of the traditional walls between school and community, school day and beyond is New York City. Over the years, New York has developed a combination of initiatives and programs that range from the Beacons, to charter schools, to strong networks of community-based organizations that have deep roots in the community and strong ties to schools.

8. Tolman, J., Pittman, K., Yohalem, N., Thomases, J., & Trammel, M. (2002). *Moving an out-of-school agenda: Lessons and challenges across cities.* Washington, DC: Forum for Youth Investment.

MERITA IRBY *is managing director of the Forum for Youth Investment and vice president of Impact Strategies, both in Washington, D.C.*

KAREN J. PITTMAN *is executive director of the Forum for Youth Investment and president of Impact Strategies, both in Washington, D.C.*

JOEL TOLMAN *is senior program associate at the Forum for Youth Investment in Washington, D.C.*

*Some learning environments show particular promise of creating pathways to postsecondary education, careers, and engaged citizenship for urban young adults from ages fifteen to twenty-four.*

# 2

# Multiple pathways to adulthood: Expanding the learning options for urban youth

*Adria Steinberg, Cheryl Almeida, Lili Allen*

FOR MOST YOUNG people, entry into high school marks the start of their transition from adolescence to adulthood. Their success at navigating this transition will determine whether by their mid-twenties, they have obtained the education and credentials to advance to a family-supporting career. Ideally, the coming-of-age years from fifteen to twenty-four are a time when young people become confident, competent learners as they solidify academic, interpersonal, and social skills. With increasing school, work, and family responsibilities, it is also a time to establish good work habits, explore future options, and develop a realistic sense of what it will take to make such options a reality.

Many young people learn a more discouraging set of lessons. They come to see secondary school as irrelevant, available jobs as demeaning, and their prospects and choices as diminishing. They find themselves moving in and out of dead-end jobs and in and out of the seemingly revolving door of postsecondary education, often

NEW DIRECTIONS FOR YOUTH DEVELOPMENT, NO. 97, SPRING 2003 © WILEY PERIODICALS, INC.

with no idea how to get from where they are to the lives they once dreamed of having.

A number of factors contribute to this diminishment of prospects, but increasingly, the aspirations of young people and their families appear to be on a collision course with what our education system seems prepared to deliver. Low-income and minority youth are likely to enter the largest and lowest-performing schools with the most inexperienced teachers, the least engaging pedagogy and curricula, and the least developed capacity to reform. In the thirty-five largest U.S. urban centers, nearly half of all high schools graduate only half of their students four years later.[1] Even many of the graduates are ill prepared for further education or employment. About a third of all graduates entering college have to take remedial classes in reading, writing, or math.[2]

Thus far, the major public response to this problem has been to focus attention and resources on improving the performance of high schools and high school students. This chapter looks at the problem, and potential solutions, through a wider-angle lens. Our assumption is that addressing the needs of young people, especially those who have not been well served by our educational system, will require the creation of multiple pathways to the skills and credentials required for a smooth transition to a productive adulthood. This makes it imperative to broaden the focus beyond schooling to learning and learning environments—both in and outside school—that are effective in helping young adults between the ages of fifteen and twenty-four traverse a pathway to further education, careers, and citizenship.

Drawing from research conducted for Jobs for the Future's *From the Margins to the Mainstream* initiative, we describe four categories of effective learning environments that show particular promise for creating such pathways for older urban youth: reinvented high schools, secondary/postsecondary blends, education/employment blends, and extended-learning opportunities.[3] We conclude by summarizing key features of these institutional arrangements and pathways and suggesting some first steps that policy and practice leaders can take to make more such environments available to young people.

## The search for effective learning environments

Two decades ago, a search for learning environments distinct from the large, impersonal high schools that are failing so many youth might have yielded a list of private or religious schools and a scattering of innovative alternative public schools and community-based youth programs. Viewed as idiosyncratic founder-driven institutions, these learning environments have long been overlooked in discussions of systemic urban high school reform. Today, however, in over a dozen cities across the United States, including New York, Boston, Sacramento, and Chicago, a smorgasbord of schools and community programs for youth are a small but increasingly accepted part of the educational landscape.

During this same period, public and civic recognition has widened regarding the role of community resources and institutions in helping to support and contribute to learning both during the school day and when young people are not in school. Fueled by growing evidence that participation in community-based youth programs promotes positive outcomes and reduces negative ones for all age groups, public-private partnerships like the 21st Century Community Learning Centers, the New York Beacons Schools, and Chicago's After School Matters are channeling new resources into large-scale youth development initiatives.

For the past several years, From the Margins to the Mainstream initiative has studied the array of places where young people gain the support, learn the skills, and obtain the credentials they need for a smooth transition to adulthood. Based on recommendations from experts in the field of youth development and education, we examined over fifty schools and programs and spoke with thirty network and intermediary leaders that help to expand the reach and impact of many of the programs. Our investigations have led us to identify four types of innovative programming that are producing strong results, especially for vulnerable youth:

*Reinvented high schools:* Small, highly focused, and rigorous learning environments that use curriculum, staff, community resources, and time in radically different ways to address the developmental as well as the intellectual growth of young people and engage them in work that matters to them and a larger community

*Secondary/postsecondary blends:* New institutional arrangements aimed at making the transition to college happen better (fewer youth fall through the cracks) and faster so that most young people have completed a first postsecondary credential by their mid-twenties

*Education/employment blends for older youth:* Programs and institutional arrangements that combine learning, technical training, and work experience, hence stepping across the usual divide between education and workforce development

*Extended learning opportunities:* Programs that make creative use of time and resources outside the usual school building and school day to engage young people in intensive learning that is potentially credit bearing (toward high school graduation)

Although these programs and schools represent a variety of institutional arrangements, all achieve results by blending the principles and best practices emerging from the youth development field with those emerging from the investigations of cognitive psychologists into the nature of learning, intelligence, and understanding. They are supported by strong and consistent evidence pointing to the effectiveness of small, personalized high schools and of community programming focused on youth development (see Figure 2.1).

Numerous studies have established links between smaller schools and a range of positive outcomes, from better attendance rates and fewer disciplinary actions to higher grades and greater satisfaction with school. Furthermore, studies have shown that these positive

## Figure 2.1. Features of effective learning environments

**Features of Learning in Successful Small Schools**
- High standards
- Focused, coherent mission
- Personalization
- Continuous cognitive challenge
- Participation

**Effective Learning Environments**

**Features of Positive Youth Development Programs**
- High expectations
- Caring relationships
- Sense of membership and belonging
- Youth voice
- Skill development

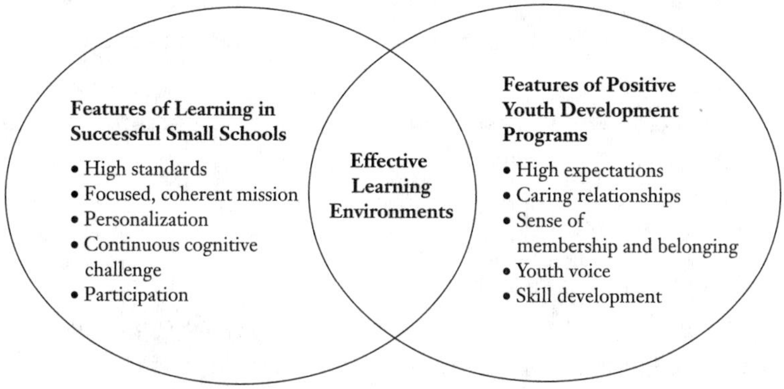

*Source:* National Research Council and Institute of Medicine. (2002). *Community programs to promote youth development* ( J. Eccles and J. A. Gootman, Eds.). Washington, DC: National Academy Press.

effects are more pronounced in schools with large concentrations of poor and minority children.[4]

A growing research base also indicates that when young people have high-quality supports and opportunities in the out-of-school hours, they do better and are better at avoiding problems.[5] Similarly, positive youth development programs are supported by several decades of research into what young people need for a successful transition to adulthood. Whether one looks at resiliency research that begins with individuals who have "beaten the odds" and works backward through what enabled them to do so, or focuses on evaluation studies that begin with key program features and look at long-term outcome data, the same basic combination of supports and opportunities emerges as critical to young people's long-term success.[6]

Our codification of these supports and opportunities led to a set of criteria for effective learning environments that we call the "5 C's":

- Caring, respectful relationships that help young people build an attachment to the learning environment and persist in the face of obstacles

- Cognitive challenges that engage young people in learning critical skills and applying those skills to complex and authentic problems
- Community membership and a sense of voice in a group where dialogue is valued
- Connections to postsecondary learning opportunities and credentials
- Culture of peer support for high-quality work

These became a shorthand for the project, offering a useful vocabulary for probing how programs organize themselves to deliver the kinds of programming codified in the 5 C's. They also became the basis for a tool to help large schools that are converting into smaller learning communities to unpack specific programming elements, key practices, and routines that will make them more effective in engaging and educating young people.[7]

## *Learning environments that blur the boundaries*

The learning environments that hold the most promise of helping vulnerable youth gain valued educational credentials cluster into the four categories of reinvented high schools, secondary/postsecondary blends, education/employment blends and extended-learning opportunities. Each of these types of programming has a key role to play in contributing to better life outcomes for urban youth. The sections below provide a more detailed look at these categories and selected examples of these schools.

### *Reinvented high schools*

Alongside incremental school improvement initiatives, a number of urban communities recently have seen the growth of more radical efforts to reinvent high school through the creation of small, more personalized, and autonomous schools of no more than four hundred students. These efforts have gained momentum with the growing public support for choice, embodied in charter legislation, local school development initiatives, and policies making it easier for money to follow the student. Indeed, some districts (among them, the Bronx in New York through the New Century Schools Initiative, the Sacramento Public Schools through the multicity Schools for a New Society Initiative, and the Chicago Public Schools through their small schools initiative) are promoting the rapid development of more such learning options. Recent and significant investments by the Carnegie Corporation of New York and the Bill and Melinda Gates Foundation are helping a growing number of cities incorporate youth development principles and new small schools into comprehensive citywide high school reform initiatives.

The goal of such systemic efforts is to make the benefits associated with small schools available to many more students. For models, reformers look to a small but growing number of reinvented high schools around the country that are creating highly focused, rigorous learning environments. These schools take advantage of their human scale (most are no larger than 350 to 400 students) to build a vibrant internal community of students and teachers, where students are known well. They also demonstrate the value of organizing time and resources outside school to increase the kinds of opportunities and supports available to young people, especially in urban environments where youth lack access to the kinds of experience that middle-class children are more likely to receive as a matter of course.

The most developed of these reinvented high schools have data showing that they are achieving positive results with students who were not successful in their previous schools. Students attend more regularly, take a more focused academic program, have better and more respectful relationships with adults, get better grades, and are more likely to graduate from high school and go on to postsecondary education in much higher numbers than comparable peers. As one research study has shown, although small schools often spend somewhat more per pupil, their low dropout rates mean that they cost less per graduate.[8]

*Examples of reinvented high schools*

Starting from a philosophy of "one student at a time," the Met, a small high school in Providence, Rhode Island, changes the nature of the learning experience by using resources and adults outside school to foster each student's cognitive and personal development. The school day, school year, and school walls are permeable, as students pursue their studies through projects accomplished in work and community settings as well as through enrolling in courses at nearby colleges.

Along with a liberal arts focus, some small schools, such as High Tech High in San Diego and the Boston Arts Academy in Boston, offer young people opportunities to specialize in an area of personal and career interest. These schools, which come to resemble high-performance work organizations, connect students with adult professionals and standards in the area of specialization.

The Horizonte Instruction and Training Center in Salt Lake City, Utah, matches each of its one thousand students to one of nine sites located throughout the community. Although students in all sites are expected to meet a common set of academic and work-readiness standards, the nature of each site varies to accommodate particular needs. For example, one site has been designed specifically for adjudicated youth and another for older youth who can attend school only part time.

*Secondary/postsecondary blends*

One of the defining features of the reinvented high schools described in this chapter is that they take direct responsibility for whether their students go to college and how they do once they are there. But the norm in most high school remains one of encouraging students to plan for their futures without doing enough to inform them of the level of skills they will need once they enter or to improve their transition from high school to college and careers. This has especially adverse affects on young people who are from families lacking contacts or familiarity with the requirements and atmosphere of higher education.

Recently, new institutional arrangements have begun to emerge that blend secondary and postsecondary education. These blended institutions begin with the premise that learning can be accelerated for adolescents and that high school and college—two separate and often not well-aligned learning environments—can be combined. The Bill and Melinda Gates Foundation, with the Carnegie Corporation of New York, the Ford Foundation, and the Kellogg Foundation, recently launched an initiative to create seventy "early colleges" within the next five years. These institutions allow young people to complete high school and earn an associate degree within a small, supportive learning environment that resembles college (and in many cases is even on a college campus) more than high school. They embody the notion that intellectual challenge and academic rigor, coupled with the opportunity to save time and tuition dollars, are powerful motivators for young people. The creation of an accelerated path to two credentials (high school and postsecondary) within a context of sustained guidance and support makes this a particularly promising model for older, vulnerable youth.

*Examples of secondary/postsecondary blends*

Portland Community College in Portland, Oregon, targets a number of programs to at-risk or out-of-school high-school-aged youth. Multiple entry points allow students with as low as third-grade-level reading skills to enroll in developmental education courses that link directly to credit-based career education programs. Once students are reading at an eighth-grade level, they enter College Bound, a program that prepares them for and links them directly into courses that count toward an associate degree. Eighty percent of the youth who enter these programs earn a diploma or general equivalency diploma (GED), return to a high school program, or obtain employment while simultaneously gaining college experience and credits.

A public secondary school chartered through a community college, Washtenaw Technical Middle College (WTMC) in Ann Arbor, Michigan, combines high school and college courses in academic and technical-vocational education so that graduating

students can earn a high school diploma and a certificate or associate degree simultaneously. Students move through five phases,
from high school core classes to credit-bearing community college courses and career pathways. WTMC students are the best-
performing group on the Washtenaw Community College
campus, with a pass rate in college courses of 80 percent.

At Okaloosa-Walton Community College Collegiate High School
in Niceville, Florida, tenth through twelfth graders can earn a
high school diploma and a two-year degree in three years. The
emphasis is on preparation for high-wage technical careers. Students who complete the dual degrees are guaranteed admission
and a scholarship for upper-division study at a Florida university and are guaranteed a seamless transfer of all their college
credits.

### Education/employment blends for older youth

Older, out-of-school, and out-of-work youth are arguably the most
neglected group of young people. Having jumped or been pushed
off the one pathway to credentials that our society recognizes and
supports—the road from a high school diploma straight to college—these young people have few options. Employment and
training programs have long represented their major safety net, yet
such programs are chronically in short supply. Furthermore, the
problem today is not just one of quantity but of quality. The new
economy has raised the bar for all youth; without some postsecondary education and training, these young people will remain
locked out of family-supporting jobs. Staying relevant to the rising
skill and credential requirements of the job market requires youth
employment programs to focus more clearly on the educational
needs and attainment of the young people they serve.

Historically, many youth employment programs have limited
their educational programming to classroom instruction in basic
competencies, geared toward a GED. However, there is a growing
consensus among experts across the fields of youth employment,
juvenile justice, education, and youth development that older youth
need comprehensive employment, training, and education leading

to postsecondary credentials with value in the labor market. A scattering of programs across the country are pioneering ways to accomplish this goal.

*Examples of education/employment blends for older youth*

At ISUS (Improved Solutions for Urban Systems—Trade and Technology Prep) in Dayton, Ohio, students, most of whom dropped out of high school, spend half their time in academic classes taught by faculty of Sinclair Community College in Dayton, Ohio, and half their time working on construction sites learning trade skills from journeymen and master craftsmen, under an arrangement with Youthbuild USA. They earn a stipend while obtaining their high school diploma, credits from Sinclair Community College, and a nationally recognized apprenticeship credential.

Created by the Southeast Los Angeles County Workforce Investment Board, the Community Youth Corps provides education, work experience and training, and supportive services to low-income young people between the ages of sixteen and twenty-one. Through partnerships with postsecondary institutions and on-site services, Community Youth Corps (CYC) offers career development paths that lead to state licenses, credentials, and college degrees. For example, through a cooperative venture with Cerritos College, CYC members may attain supervised employment and academic credit toward an early childhood education credential. The credit allows CYC youth to be cross-referred to the University of California at Los Angeles and California State University Dominguez Hills for articulation into bachelor's and master's degree programs.[9]

A thirteenth-year program for young people who completed high school but have few employment prospects, Year-Up uses a combination of classroom instruction and corporate internships to prepare them for immediate entry into well-paid technical positions, as well as for further learning in a college setting. The program started in Boston and is expanding to other cities.

## Extended-learning opportunities

As young people reach middle and older adolescence, what they need and look for in the after-school hours changes. While younger children need a safe, supervised environment with a mix of recreation, educational activities, and homework help, adolescents require a different mix. They need these hours to be replete with engaging and purposeful learning opportunities.[10]

In the past decade, urban high schools have begun to limit their offerings to core academic subjects in response to tightened budgets and heightened pressure to raise the percentages of students who can meet state standards.[11] As the high school hones in on a defined set of academic skills, the after-school hours are taking on increased importance as the time for young people to develop civic, vocational, and social skills and to explore interests and passions that can lead them to a sense of purpose in their high school studies and their pursuit of postsecondary options.

Low-income young people need what middle-class young people get as a matter of course from their schools and communities. Middle-class youth can count on an enriched set of electives in school, as well as a full complement of extracurricular activities, private lessons, travel opportunities, summer learning experiences, and the like. For low-income young people attending large, impersonal high schools with a streamlined academic focus, extended learning opportunities can help to close this gap. They need both formal and informal opportunities in the twelve or so waking hours each day they spend outside school settings to gain skills and develop interests that can help them advance toward postsecondary education and credentials.

Although small in size and number, a scattering of high-quality programs around the country are effective in using time and resources outside the usual school building and school day to engage young people in intensive, purposeful learning that connects them with their futures. The best of these programs hook young people by appealing to their passions and giving them opportunities for meaningful connection to their communities and for internships that combine work and learning. A small number have begun to work on credentialing out-of-school learning.

*Examples of extended-learning opportunities*

Chicago's Gallery 37 offers young people job training in the arts, opportunities for arts-related employment, and mentoring relationships with professional artists. Gallery 37 began its programming as a single-site summer program in 1991 and now offers year-round after-school arts apprenticeship programs in schools and community-based organizations to about forty-eight hundred youth annually.

Located in community organizations, Youth Voices in Philadelphia structures community-based research projects for young people in which students learn critical thinking, computer, and research skills, as well as important leadership skills. Acting as mentors and teachers, university students, who often come from the same neighborhoods as the program participants, help their protégés to act as researchers and community activists and to see the college experience as something within their reach.

City Links, a public sector apprenticeship program for recent immigrant students in Cambridge, Massachusetts connects an in-school credit-bearing course in government, leadership, and immigration history to after-school jobs in the public sector and a weekly after-school seminar on employability skills. All activities are counted for the course credit.

## Conclusion

The programs described here represent a range of institutional arrangements and programming types. Those showing the most promise of accelerating the advancement of vulnerable youth share the following characteristics:

- The flexibility to customize the learning environment to match the career goals, interests and passions, and life circumstances of the young person
- The authorization to grant credits toward a diploma or postsecondary credential with value in the marketplace

- A focus on young people producing high-quality work that meets real-world standards
- A literacy focus that balances basic skills with purposeful communication
- The institutional agility to access and orchestrate the range of supports and opportunities the young person needs

Despite their promise, many of these programs remain on the margins. Underfunded and politically vulnerable, they struggle to survive and grow. The challenge is to develop policies that keep pace with and accelerate programmatic innovation so that a strong mix of effective learning environments, both in and outside school, becomes typical of the educational experiences of all young people coming of age, especially in our nation's cities.

An important first step for policymakers is to take seriously the emerging evidence about small schools and community youth development and the substantive programmatic innovation on which it is based. By making a greater investment in such schools and programs, policymakers can immediately increase the quantity and quality of effective learning environments available to young people.

The opportunity also exists in many cities to use the lessons from innovative programming and models to reform high school. As cities across the country initiate high school reform initiatives, there is also an important opening to use what is being learned on the margins, where innovation is most likely to take place. Cities that are already investing in the conversion of large high schools into small learning communities can protect that investment by drawing on the knowledge and expertise developed in effective small schools and youth programs.

Ultimately, the value of innovative programming goes far beyond its usefulness in infiltrating new ideas into the mainstream. The lessons of these "existence proofs" for personalized and engaged learning can also help cities to envision their way to a new mainstream. If young people are to emerge from the coming-of-age years as full participants in our society and economy, they need access to a variety of high-quality, developmentally and culturally responsive learning options that individually and collectively improve and accelerate their transition to college and careers. The effective learning environments on the margins of our one-size-fits-all high schools provide our best clues to the kinds of institutions and institutional arrangements that should be part of a redefined system of secondary education.

### Notes

1. Balfantz, R., & Legters, N. (2001). *How many central city high schools have a severe dropout problem, where are they located, and who attends them? Initial estimates using the common core of data*. Cambridge, MA: Harvard University Graduate School of Education and Achieve.

2. Cloud, J. (2002, Oct. 14). Who's ready for college? *Time*, 60–63.

3. From the Margins to the Mainstream seeks practical answers to the question of how communities can take advantage of breakthrough possibilities offered by emerging, powerful learning environments—inside and outside the school building, school day, and school year. It seeks to develop policies and practices that increase the impact and visibility of learning environments that succeed in getting young people onto a pathway to high school diplomas and college-level studies and engage them in contributing to their communities. The initiative is supported by grants from the Carnegie Corporation of New York, the John D. and Catherine T. MacArthur Foundation, the W. K. Kellogg Foundation, the Charles Stewart Mott Foundation, and Atlantic Philanthropies.

4. Gladden, R. (1998). *The small school movement: A review of the literature*. In M. Fine & J. I. Somerville (Eds.), *Small schools, big imaginations: A creative look at urban school reform*. Chicago: Cross City Campaign for Urban School Reform; Howley, C., Strange, M., & Bickel, R. (2000). *Research about school size and school performance in impoverished communities*. Charleston, WV: ERIC Clearinghouse on Rural Education and Small Schools (ED 448 968); Lee, V. E. (2000). School size and the organization of secondary schools. In M. T. Hallinan (Ed.), *2000 handbook of the sociology of education*. New York: Kluwer Academic/Plenum; Raywid, M. A. (1996). *Taking stock: The movement to create mini-schools, schools-within-schools, and separate small schools*. Madison, WI: Center on Organization and Restructuring of Schools.

5. Scales, P. C., & Leffert, N. (1999). *Development assets: A synthesis of the scientific research on adolescent development*. Minneapolis, MN: Search Institute.

6. National Research Council and Institute of Medicine. (2002). *Community programs to promote youth development* (J. Eccles & J. A. Gootman, Eds.). Washington, DC: National Academy Press.

7. This tool appears in Steinberg, A., & Allen, L. (2002). *From large to small: Strategies for personalizing the high school*. Boston: Jobs for the Future. Available on-line: www.jff.org/Margins/Index/html.

8. Stiefel, L., Iatarola, P., Fruchter, N., & Berne, R. (1998). *The effects of size of student body on school costs and performance in NY City high schools.* New York: New York University Institute for Education and Social Policy.

9. The descriptions of ISUS Trade and Technology and the Community Youth Corps are based on Abdulezer, S. (2001). It's a wonderful life! *Converge, 4.* Available on-line: www.convergemag.com; National Youth Employment Coalition PEPNet 2002 Awards; www.nyec.org/pepnet/awardees/cyc.htm.

10. McLaughlin, M. (1999). *Community counts: How youth organizations matter for youth development.* Washington, DC: Public Education Network; Tolman, J., Pittman, K., Yohalem, N., Thomases, J., & Trammel, M. (2002). *Moving an out-of-school agenda: Lessons and challenges across cities.* Washington, DC: Forum for Youth Investment.

11. Meier, D. (2002). Standardization versus standards. *Phi Delta Kappan, 84*(3), 190–198.

ADRIA STEINBERG *is program director at Jobs for the Future in Boston, Massachusetts.*

CHERYL ALMEIDA *is research fellow at Jobs for the Future in Boston, Massachusetts.*

LILI ALLEN *is research fellow at Jobs for the Future in Boston, Massachusetts.*

*Local education funds can effectively engage their communities to align resources, policies, and public will to provide children and youth with supportive learning environments.*

# 3

# Building learning-centered communities through public engagement

*Richard Tagle*

IN LINCOLN, NEBRASKA, the Lincoln Public Schools Foundation (LPSF), working alongside the 21st Century Community Learning Center Office and other municipal departments, is paving the way to provide over five thousand public school students with expanded learning opportunities, after-school activities, and a wide array of programs and supports through the establishment of community learning centers (CLCs). LPSF, a local education fund (LEF), and its partners envisioned school-based CLCs as an appropriate mechanism to address the growing health and social service needs of poor children and youth, to close the achievement gap between minority and nonminority students, and to foster community involvement in school improvement efforts.[1] They are laying the groundwork to guarantee that all of Lincoln's children and youth will have equal access to quality public education and to supports and programs provided by other local agencies working in collaboration with schools.

NEW DIRECTIONS FOR YOUTH DEVELOPMENT, NO. 97, SPRING 2003 © WILEY PERIODICALS, INC.

Four other LEFs are leading the way in providing children and youth with programs, supports, and opportunities for enhanced learning and development in their communities. In Pennsylvania, the Lancaster Foundation for Education Enrichment is collaborating with the Network for Safe and Healthy Children to create family resource centers within the Lancaster Public Schools. In New Jersey, the Paterson Education Fund is holding public dialogues to gather community input on how to transform the city's public schools into full-service community schools. In Providence, Rhode Island, the Public Education Fund is helping to establish an extended community center within the only public elementary school in the Olneyville neighborhood. The Education Fund for Greater Buffalo in New York is engaging both adults and youth in incorporating community space within schools that will be constructed or renovated within the next five years.

All of these activities are part of Public Education Network's (PEN) Schools and Community Initiative (funded by the Annenberg Foundation) to provide a comprehensive and coordinated set of supports and programs that ensure children's success in school and in their communities.[2] The initiative's goal is to help local communities align resources, programs, and collaborative partnerships, such as those between schools and community-based agencies, toward children's learning and development.

## The need for learning-centered communities

The five LEFs involved in the Schools and Community Initiative are implementing activities that engage the public in linking public schools with community-based programs and creating opportunities for children and youth to grow, learn, and develop in their communities. They are finding ways to transform public schools into more than just facilities for academic learning and exploring how other local institutions can play a role in providing academic and nonacademic supports for students before, during, and after school hours. They are, in essence, creating unified and local visions for the way children and youth learn and develop by redefining the ways schools, community-based organizations, and other stakeholders work and collaborate.

In an era of high standards, schools are pressed to focus strictly on their academic mission. In the words of Anthony Alvarado, chancellor of instruction at San Diego Public Schools, "There has to be a massive attempt to change school systems into communities that generate practice, focused on what kids need to learn and be able to do. There is no other agenda."[3] However, researchers agree that children and youth learn in various ways, in various venues, and in times beyond the school hours. In addition, they need supports and programs, and if these are unavailable, their achievement in the classroom could be hindered. As the stakes for public schools increase, educators and others face the dilemma of how to address the nonacademic needs of children without distracting schools from reaching their academic goals.

Families, peers, civic leaders, mentors, and other community members all contribute to the achievement of children's learning outcomes. In many communities, children face significant barriers to learning that schools alone cannot possibly overcome.[4] In partnership with schools, other community institutions help ensure academic and social success by addressing children's basic needs, such as proper nutrition, good health, and safe environments. Strategies to address these needs and other supports range from using the school facility as a hub for services rendered (school-based services) to linking the school with other local providers through site coordinators or liaisons.

According to the National Research Council, schools and communities in the past supported and enhanced young people's development. But social forces dramatically changed this landscape.[5] Now, more than ever before, schools and communities must work together to provide a strong base of support for young people as they grow into adulthood. Strong school and community connections are especially critical in poor, disadvantaged communities where schools often are the largest piece of public real estate and may be the single largest employer.[6] Efforts to create a comprehensive approach to address children's needs must extend beyond collaboration between schools and community-based groups. Providing comprehensive and coordinated supports for children and youth should be centered on a communitywide and community-owned vision of learning, development, and well-being supported by cohesive and sustainable policy and effective practice.

Learning-centered communities consider the achievement and success of children and youth to be the ultimate outcome of their collaborative work. PEN defines achievement and success more broadly, encompassing both academic and nonacademic outcomes. Learning-centered communities work to ensure that all children meet high academic standards, develop a sense of civic duty and community connection, and acquire the capacity for lifelong learning. In this vein, schools, churches, neighborhoods, families, and other community institutions all work together to align resources, assets, talents, and opportunities with the needs of children, youth, and their families.

## The role of public engagement

The process of transforming schools and community into environments for enhanced learning and development is not an easy task. More than establishing programs, investing funds, and hiring personnel, PEN's Schools and Community Initiative focuses on the sustainability of effective practice and policy that support school and community collaboration regardless of changing local demographics, social context, and political landscape. Public engagement is an essential ingredient of long-term sustainability (see Chapter One, this volume). But public engagement is defined in various ways by different entities. Some define it in terms of the willingness of citizens to invest financial resources, time, and energy toward a specific project or issue.[7] This willingness reflects a commitment to public education and the belief that public education is worth the personal and social investment needed to sustain it.

Others define engagement in terms of communication, or the process by which schools and communities engage in a two-way dialogue to solve problems and support improvement.[8] For example, Public Agenda, a national public opinion research organization, emphasizes extensive outreach, discussions geared to average citizens, a civil exchange of ideas, and tolerance for different points of view in its public engagement approach.[9]

Another way of looking at public engagement is through grassroots organizing. Community organizers see that leadership, action, and reform can begin at the grassroots level. Major campaigns, whether around housing, jobs, or education, are designed to reach the unorganized majority of low- and moderate-income people who are the key constituency to be mobilized for progressive movement toward change.[10] Community organizing is a mechanism through which marginalized voices are heard and the community at large becomes a critical stakeholder.

## *PEN's framework for public engagement*

Social investment, dialogue, and community organizing are essential elements of effective and authentic public engagement. Undergirding the Schools and Community Initiative is PEN's framework for public engagement, a theory of action that includes a commitment to engage multiple constituencies, from opinion leaders and policymakers to the general, sometimes disenfranchised public. PEN believes that when all constituencies in a community take responsibility for public schools, not only will there be policy change; there will also be a stronger civic infrastructure, an increased local capacity to solve problems, a more vibrant economic life, and more citizens fully participating in a democratic society. This is represented by the following equation:

Public engagement + specific school reform goals
= Sustained policy and practice
+ public responsibility.

PEN defines *public* in this equation as three distinct audiences:

*The community at large:* All residents of a community, including parents, school district employees, and other community members,
especially those who traditionally have been excluded from community discussion or may not truly be represented by an organized stakeholder group.

*Organized stakeholder groups:* Groups with an interest in education
that are formally organized to represent others and wield influence with policymakers. These can include, but are not limited
to, chambers of commerce, parent-teacher associations, teacher
unions, higher education institutions, faith-based organizations,
service providers, and other locally based civic organizations.

*Policymakers:* Elected and appointed officials with direct authority
to make legislative or regulatory policy or to allocate resources
for schools, such as legislators, governors, state school board
members, chief state school officers, mayors, city councils,
boards of education, and superintendents.

These audiences, or publics, are engaged through a set of intertwined strategies:

*Community organizing:* LEFs, through partnerships with other local
organizing entities, sponsor grassroots organizing activities such as
neighborhood meetings and door-to-door visits that give community residents and others a chance to share opinions, shape decisions,
and take responsibility for the success of a program or approach.

*Strategic planning:* LEFs take the lead in convening and facilitating
a communitywide process to develop comprehensive plans on
how to reach community-developed goals. The strategic planning
process is organized around the formal involvement of stakeholder groups and school district leaders, but is also influenced by
the policymaking environment and the community at large.

*Advocacy for policy and practice change:* LEFs work with partner organizations to advocate with local and state policymakers to address
barriers to the effective implementation of local strategic plans

or to take advantage of opportunities to accelerate their completion and effectiveness. LEFs in this case help identify the barriers and opportunities that become the fodder for state-level advocacy. They can also take positions on specific legislation and urge others with similar views to do the same.

## How public engagement helps to build a learning-centered community

Given this framework, how does public engagement enable schools and community to expand its capacity to address the learning and development needs of children and youth? How can an engaged public help broaden the definition of success for children and youth and align its resources and institutions to help create learning-centered communities?

LEFs know that engaging the public early in the initiative process allows them to identify and clarify pressing issues and problems that should be addressed. In conducting a survey of parents and other caregivers in the Lancaster school district, LFEE discovered that families are very much concerned about the safety of their children in school. No matter what project they undertake, it must incorporate the issue of safe and healthy school environments. In Paterson, the Paterson Education Fund heard clearly from community forum participants that public schools need to have space for community programs and services. This input coincides with a state government allocation of over $12 billion in school construction funding over the next ten years to address the growing problem of overcrowded and deteriorating school facilities. In Lincoln, LPSF found out that Nebraska is the state with the highest proportion of working mothers, thus clarifying the need for afterschool programs to meet the state's child care needs. There are a myriad of ways through which schools and communities can begin addressing the needs of children and youth. Engaging the public early in the process paves the way for the prioritization of activities and available resources.

Engaging stakeholders enables schools and community to maximize existing resources. There may not be sufficient local or state funds allocated for family resource centers or community learning centers, but by engaging community-based agencies and other municipal sectors, LEFs discover that various entities are able to contribute time, personnel, and funds toward slices of a larger endeavor. In Lincoln, CLC staff are largely funded through a federal 21st Century Community Learning Center grant. But many of the programs and supports provided are funded by community-based service agencies such as the YMCA, United Way, and Family Services. In Buffalo, the Education Fund for Greater Buffalo uses funding from a community foundation to engage youth in identifying policies and practices to be incorporated in the design of community schools. The actual development of these community schools is supported with funds from the mayor's office and the United Way. In Providence, the Public Education Fund initiative to transform an elementary school into an extended full-service school is augmented by funds from the Olneyville Neighborhood Revitalization program.

Public engagement, as a process, also increases the capacity of policymakers to respond to public demand and need. As LEFs and their partners build a broad constituency for the learning and development of children and youth, policymakers will recognize a growing public demand. In all initiative sites, local collaboratives have discovered that categorical funding is a hindrance to effective coordination of services and programs. This is communicated to municipal and state leaders who in turn direct their state department heads to allow more flexibility in funding programs. The Paterson Education Fund is working with the Education Law Center to get the state government to provide funds for supplemental and support services to high-poverty schools to help poor students meet high academic standards. In Nebraska, state legislators are looking at various ways to pool resources to allow CLCs to flourish throughout the state. In Lancaster, local advocates are working with state agencies to examine ways in which Title 1 funds can be used to coordinate support services provided through family resource centers. Through effective public engagement, policy-makers are included in the processes that effect change, and local community institutions have greater traction in their collaboration.

As LEFs organize residents and other community members, and new structures for voicing and sharing opinions are created, new leaders and new players emerge. The Education Fund for Greater Buffalo used the issue of finance equity, a hot topic throughout the state due to the recent state supreme court ruling stating that the current state education funding is unconstitutional, to engage students in a public debate. Students in grades 7 through 12 engaged in a public debate, which was broadcast live on public television, on whether Buffalo public schools get their fair share of funds from the state government and if these funds are sufficient to ensure that all children in the Buffalo school district can meet high state standards. In Providence, the Public Education Fund gathered the opinions and views of Olneyville residents on how to improve access to children's health services. Their views were then incorporated into a plan to transform an elementary school into a full-service community school. Some Olneyville residents were tapped to serve on the advisory group charged with monitoring progress of the transformation.

## Challenges in engaging the public

Public engagement also poses both conceptual and practical challenges to LEFs and their partners. LEFs, for the most part, needed to recognize that public engagement is both a process and an outcome of their initiative efforts. If LEFs were able to change policy and practice without community involvement, they would not have met the goals of the initiative. On the other hand, public engagement requires a long period of time; those who are accustomed to seeing quick results and outcomes can be frustrated by slow progress.

Engaging the public also means being able to speak in commonly understood language. "Learning and development" mean different things to different audiences, and LEFs are often in a quandary to find ways by which concepts and messages can be presented in a universal fashion. In Lincoln, for example, LPSF is implementing a major communications and media campaign to build common understanding of the concept of community learning centers as more than just after-school programs. The Paterson Education Fund has cosponsored a statewide conference with the Coalition for Our Children's Schools to get key players and partners to gain a common understanding of community schools.

"Turfism" surfaces as a threat to fully engaging the public. Nothing scares off stakeholders more than the notion of putting their resources into a pot to which others have access. Schools and community-based organizations often see themselves as having their own set of tools, funds, and results for which they are separately accountable. Some pundits assert that community engagement only slows the progress that educators could make and that community-based organizations diffuse the decision-making process that would lead to educational improvement and results.[11] Community-based providers counter that schools have a closed-door policy that prevents connections to children and youth needing nonacademic supports. LEFs have been in the middle of this tug-of-war since their creation in the early 1980s. As traditional conveners and brokers, LEFs are able to mediate dialogues between school districts and other community sectors to create an environment conducive for collaboration. In Buffalo, the Education Fund of Greater Buffalo sits on the school board's school construction committee giving community input to board decisions. In Lancaster, the Lancaster Fund for Education Enrichment, as a liaison between the superintendent's office and the Network for Safe and Healthy Children, identifies opportunities for the network to contribute to the school district's strategic plan. In turn, fund identifies ways the school district can help support the network in building safe and healthy environments for school children.

Related to turfism is the public notion of the traditional institutional roles that schools and community service providers play. Many see schools merely as academic centers whose mission is solely to ensure high academic achievement and community health centers merely as places that address the health needs and concerns of local residents. Libraries provide books, museums record history, and police ensure community safety and prevent crime. Getting these entities to redefine their work based on how they could contribute to learning and development of a child is a major task. LEFs play a major role in looking at the broader landscape and being able to identify various local assets and resources, regardless of where they originate, that can be tapped to pursue a unified vision for learning. Hence, schools become more than just academic centers. They become hubs that coordinate various supports. Libraries become reading and learning centers, museums become venues for service-learning, and police become mentors to young adults.

## Role of LEFs

LEFs have been playing the role of conveners and brokers on behalf of the school district and the community for over twenty years. Although many were formed to generate private and public funds to help with school reform, LEFs have expanded their activities into whole school reform, policy change, and, now, communitywide engagement. Given their structure as nonprofit community-based organizations, independent from their school districts and with boards that are reflective of the communities they serve, LEFs are "set up to be fast-moving, nimble, non-bureaucratic, and able to take on areas of work that posed greater organizational or political challenges to large and inflexible school bureaucracies."[12]

LEFs are in a unique position to help create learning-centered communities. They have addressed the issue of trust and turf through twenty years of credible work on behalf of school districts and the poor communities they serve. Local agencies in Lincoln point to the Lincoln Public School Foundation's previous work in school health and library improvements as the source of the LEF's credibility in the community. The Education Fund for Greater Buffalo's creation of a youth advocacy council garnered the trust and support of several youth-serving agencies.

By being able to leverage resources that support school-community collaboration, LEFs are seen as key players in the success of such endeavors. The five LEFs involved in the Schools and Community Initiative have been able to collectively raise $2.1 million in local, private dollars in addition to the $2.5 million in grants PEN provided over a three-year period. Averaging almost $1 million in grant funds per site, LEFs were able to augment school-community partnerships and therefore gain the support and attention of other key players.

With resources in hand, LEFs can also help community-wide initiatives by providing the opportunity for incubator and pilot programs. The Lancaster Foundation for Educational Enrichment, for example, is using its PEN grant to help the community and the school district address the dire need for family resource centers. Although existing resources are not sufficient to do this on a districtwide scale, the foundation was able to set up pilot family resource centers in three elementary schools. What they learn as these centers are established, implemented, and evaluated will help future plans to establish family resource centers throughout the school district.

Through their connection with PEN, LEFs also become conduits for local-national learning. PEN provides technical assistance, ranging from program design to fundraising to organizational development, not only to the initiative sites but to all PEN members through its membership services department. Within the Schools and Community Initiative, this assistance is also extended to the LEF's local partners; the community therefore benefits not just from the monetary grant but also from the technical assistance it receives. PEN also brings national attention and interest to the accomplishments and challenges of these communities by promoting the work in newsletters, on listservs, at conferences, and in publications.

Data are another tool that LEFs use to engage various publics fully. They conduct polls, surveys, and other assessment activities to get the pulse of the community in terms of assets, needs, knowledge, and capacity. LEFs also gather and analyze school data and present them to the public in lay terms. By combining school and community data, LEFs can present a clear local picture of the conditions that children and youth face: their academic performance, health status, general well-being, available and needed supports, and even their dreams and aspirations.

Having both financial resources and data in their grasp, LEFs are able to do what school districts and other community-based providers often cannot: ask the hard questions. LEFs can pose issues of race, class, and gender equity to schools and communities. They can hold public dialogues around the equitable allocation of resources, accountability of elected leaders and officials, and the willingness of key stakeholders to work together on behalf of all children and youth.

Finally, with their participation in the Schools and Community Initiative, a new role has emerged for LEFs: that of local and statewide advocacy. Having scanned the landscape of school-community work, gathered data about how children succeed and perform, and gained the support and involvement of a broad constituency, LEFs now see themselves as entities able to deliver a community message to local and state policymakers. LEFs are becoming more articulate on how the worlds of school and community merge into a seamless support system and how these connections contribute not just to children's academic and social achievement, but also to community development. LEFs are able to see how local and state policies can support their work and promote practices that are sustained and ingrained into local norms and culture.

## Conclusion

LEFs are able to navigate the rough waters of school reform and social change. Their structure and the scope of their work allow them to link various sectors and facilitate cooperation and collaboration among them. LEFs are then able to redefine and recreate the environments in which children and youth learn, grow into productive adulthood, and become contributing citizens of their communities. As of this writing, the Lincoln Public Schools Foundation and its partners created a governance structure for their community-learning centers. Called the *leadership team*, this body is composed of various community representatives: school board, mayor's office, service providers, funders, parents, teachers, and young people themselves. In 2000, the partnership began with three CLCs. Their work has now expanded to include fifteen CLCs with a long-term plan of transforming all of Lincoln's fifty public schools into community learning centers. Envisioning a community that supports its residents from cradle to grave, the LEF and its partners are leading the effort to define success and achievement for all children and youth broadly.

## Notes

1. Local education funds are nonprofit, community-based organizations dedicated to increasing student achievement in public schools and building broad-based support for quality public education.
2. Public Education Network's mission is to build public demand and mobilize resources for quality public education through a constituency of individuals and local education funds.
3. Alvarado, A. (1998, Nov.). *Improving the power of teacher learning*. Address to the Public Education Network Annual Conference, Washington, DC.
4. Dryfoos, J., & McGuire, S. (2000). *Inside full service community schools*. Thousand Oaks, CA: Corwin Press.
5. National Research Council. (2002). *Community programs to promote youth development*. Washington, DC: National Academy Press.
6. Adelman, H. H., & Taylor, L. (2001). *School-community partnerships: A guide*. Los Angeles: UCLA Center for Mental Health in Schools, University of California at Los Angeles.
7. Voke, H. (2002). *Engaging the public in its schools*. Washington, DC: Association of Supervision and Curriculum Development.
8. National Education Association. (2002). *Engaging the public in public education* [brochure]. Washington, DC: National Education Association.
9. Public Agenda Online. (2002). *Public engagement programs: How we engage the public*. Available on-line: www.publicagenda.org.
10. Association of Community Organizations for Reform Now. (2002). *Who is Acorn?* Available on-line: http:acorn.org/whoisacorn/index.html.
11. Public Education Network. (2002). *Lessons from the field: Policy initiatives planning phase*. Washington, DC: Public Education Network.
12. Useem, E. (1999). *From the margins to the center of school reform: A look at the work of local education funds in seventeen communities*. Washington, DC: Public Education Network.

RICHARD TAGLE *is a senior associate and manager of the Schools and Community Initiative for the Public Education Network in Washington, D.C.*

*This article proposes a strategy for the use of out-of-school time for adolescents, illustrates this strategy in action in Chicago, and discusses the challenges it faces.*

# 4

# High school after school: Creating pathways to the future for adolescents

*Joan R. Wynn*

THROUGH LEGISLATION, financing, and action, a groundswell of attention is aimed at increasing student achievement and harnessing the out-of-school hours to this goal. For adolescents, much of the debate has been focused on the negative consequences of overlooking the nonschool hours.[1] Little attention has been given to the specific value and use of out-of-school time for teenagers or to a debate about whether or in what ways it should advance an academic agenda.

This chapter proposes a strategy for using out-of-school time so that it operates as a system of opportunities for adolescents. This strategy integrates and extends existing programs and resources provided by community-based organizations, public institutions, and the business sector to provide a series of graduated opportunities for engagement, learning, and contribution.

NEW DIRECTIONS FOR YOUTH DEVELOPMENT, NO. 97, SPRING 2003 © WILEY PERIODICALS, INC.

## Positive pathways for adolescents

A system of this kind should include four kinds of opportunities that together can provide positive pathways to the future for adolescents: opportunities for participation in engaging activities, apprenticeships with skilled professionals, work-site internships, and part-time and summer jobs (see Figure 4.1).

These pathway opportunities should enable youth to identify and pursue interests (or, better yet, passions), apply what they are learning in ways that benefit others, and receive increasing responsibility and recognition. Together, they should build on and acknowledge learning that occurs both in and out of school in order to stimulate interest, inquiry, and mastery, not to narrow youth interests or channel them into particular careers.

While creating a system of this kind will take substantial, sustained attention to adolescents, defining what this system looks like can guide ways to integrate and extend the resources now invested in youth. Examples of this strategy in action later in this chapter will ground it in real work now underway.

### Participation

Opportunities for participation can introduce youth to a variety of engaging activities—artistic and athletic, civic and cultural, and others. These opportunities should be broadly available, support constructive use of out-of-school time, enable youth to participate in activities they like to do—to have fun—and identify or deepen interests and abilities. Ultimately, the kinds and quantity of opportunities for participation should enable all youth to find activities

**Figure 4.1. A pathway of opportunities**

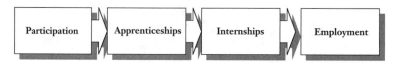

that matter to them, which they want to learn more about and become good at.

## Apprenticeships

Apprenticeships should be hands-on, interactive opportunities in specific topics, like Web design, robotics, African drumming, and textile design, that enable small groups of youth to work intensively with professionals who are skilled in their craft and interested in helping teenagers find productive pathways to the future. These opportunities can enable adolescents to pursue interests, develop and deepen skills, and use these skills to benefit others.

Apprenticeships should give youth opportunities to apply their increasing knowledge and skills in products, performances, and other concrete contributions. And they can recognize participants' increasing abilities and contributions by paying stipends and awarding credit toward high school graduation. Compensation and credit can reinforce learning in and out of school; they also can create complexities, which are discussed at the end of this chapter.

## Internships

Internships should build on skills gained in apprenticeships, provide instruction and learning experiences in a work setting, and offer exposure to work expectations and environments. Organizations of different kinds, sizes, and locations can sponsor internships, including nonprofits (from local community organizations to major hospitals and universities), government agencies (from local schools and parks to central offices of city, county, and other public agencies), and businesses (in local neighborhoods and in downtown locations).

Internships move youth from an experience in which a professional comes to work with them in a group to an environment in which they are learning in and contributing to a working organization. They introduce youth to the expectations and obligations of work and enable them to develop evolving skills. Because internships are primarily learning experiences, interns can be paid stipends that cover the costs of participating, such as food and transportation.

### Employment

As part of this system of opportunities, adolescents should have an opportunity for paid employment in part-time or summer jobs before they graduate from high school. These jobs should build on past experiences and contributions and further introduce youth to the requirements and rewards of paid employment. Ideally, these jobs should not reproduce the often-routinized work available to teenagers, which isolates them from adults and reinforces disengagement.[2]

Paid employment for adolescents is not meant to tip the balance between education and employment. Beyond moderate amounts, too much employment, like too much unstructured time, is linked to negative consequences for youth.[3] Like other pathway opportunities, engaging jobs with reasonable time commitments, rather than distract from school, can enhance the relevance of education and the determination to pursue it.

### What these opportunities amount to

Together, these opportunities for youth—participation, apprenticeships, internships, and employment—share a number of defining characteristics. Currently, youth have limited exposure through school or the media to the kinds of occupations to which they can aspire. Cumulatively, pathway opportunities can connect adolescents to skilled professionals in an array of occupations and help them understand the pathways these adults have pursued.

Creating a system of out-of-school opportunities of this kind can also develop connections for youth between home, school, and neighborhood settings and opportunities located farther afield. The chance to pursue interests in downtown locations, from participation to employment, can introduce youth to a world of broader prospects and a wider network of connections. In both formal and informal ways, these connections can enable young people to garner information about this world and how to navigate in it. As important, youth can meet people—program staff, internship instructors, employers—who have information about next-step opportunities and contacts young people can tap.

These pathway opportunities were described in a linear way as taking youth in sequence from participation to employment. But it is important to note that youth can and should be free to create pathways that are not linear. Youth can be involved in different kinds and levels of activities at the same time and over time. Depending on inclinations and other obligations, they can be engaged in multiple opportunities to participate at a given time or involved in paid employment in one area and first-time participants in another.

Developing a system of opportunities for youth is not meant to value one kind of opportunity above others; rather, the intent is to enable youth to pursue interests, use increasing knowledge and skills to contribute in ways that matter to them and to adults around them, and have increasing responsibility and recognition in meaningful endeavors while in high school.

Through these opportunities, young people can develop and deepen specific content knowledge and know-how. In addition, they can acquire the kinds of soft skills—leadership, decision making, negotiating, and working as part of a group—that are important for participating effectively in education, employment, and civic life.

Together, these opportunities provide real-world occasions to demonstrate what youth know and can do, characteristics that are key to youth engagement and to consolidating the knowledge and skills they gain. In this way, these out-of-school opportunities share characteristics and learning benefits similar to project-based and service-learning and to schools that are situating learning in settings outside building walls.

### Connecting youth to opportunities

Developing sufficient high-quality opportunities is critical. But these opportunities will not operate as a system without ways of informing youth about and increasing access to them.

In part because out-of-school opportunities have not been seen or functioned as a sector, information about opportunities for youth in the out-of-school hours is often hard to find. For youth in low-income neighborhoods, local opportunities are often limited, and many youth do not have the personal networks through which their more advantaged peers can learn about a citywide arts program, access business internships, find a first summer job, or learn about colleges and college scholarships.

Absent personal networks, young people need ways to get themselves noticed by opportunities in which they are interested. At present, the only record of a young person's achievements is a high school transcript (primarily course grades). The experiences, responsibilities, and achievements youth gain in the out-of-school hours are unrecorded. Developing an inventory of out-of-school opportunities and a record of out-of-school experience and achievement is part of creating a citywide system of pathways to the future for adolescents.

## Bringing this strategy to life

It is possible that the use of out-of-school time by adolescents may gain increased attention, driven by a number of intersecting policy agendas, including high-stakes pressures to increase academic achievement, welfare reform and its recently identified negative effects on adolescents, increased investment in the after-school hours even in a time of fiscal constraint, and interest in youth risk reduction and workforce preparation.

Aspects of a system of out-of-school opportunities for adolescents already exist to some extent in the opportunities paid for and provided by public agencies, including schools, community-based organizations, and businesses. Aligning and extending these resources can provide the basis on which a system of graduated opportunities for adolescents can be built. In Chicago, a major initiative is underway to do just this.

After School Matters (ASM) is a public-private collaboration that is working to create a citywide system of out-of-school opportunities for adolescents in Chicago. Working with the City of Chicago, nonprofit organizations, and businesses, ASM is spearheading the development of a system of graduated opportunities of the kind described above.

After School Matters is developing this system by pursuing three core strategies:

- Working to create a comprehensive network of out-of-school opportunities that mobilizes and builds on what exists
- Pursuing both a neighborhood-based and a citywide strategy
- Enlisting key sectors—government, youth-serving organizations, businesses, and others—to significantly increase and align their contributions in order to create a sustainable infrastructure of quality opportunities

In pursuing these strategies, ASM is committed to serving as an engine and honest broker, creating partnerships among those who provide opportunities and those who can generate the resources, assistance, and accountability to enable them to operate at a scale that makes a difference.

*Origins and early history*

After School Matters builds on and expands Gallery 37, Chicago's respected and widely replicated arts apprenticeship program for young people in the visual, literary, media, culinary, and performing arts.[4] Begun in 1990, Gallery 37 offers young people mentoring relationships with professional artists, training in the arts, and opportunities for arts-related employment. In the process, youth produce artwork for public installation, performance, publication, and sale. Maggie Daley, wife of Chicago's mayor, was instrumental in creating Gallery 37. She proposed and is leading the development of ASM.

In its neighborhood-based approach, ASM locates activities around clusters of a high school, park, and library that serve as a single campus for programming. Each cluster leverages the resources of the schools, parks, and libraries—funding, facilities, and staff—and makes them available for more extensive programs over extended hours. In each cluster, staff who work for the schools, parks, libraries, community-based organizations, and businesses organize and lead ASM programs.

After School Matters is working most intensively in low-performing high schools and in neighborhoods with few existing opportunities for youth. Originally in six neighborhoods in the fall of 2000, ASM is now working in eighteen racially and ethnically diverse low-income neighborhoods in Chicago. Through its partnerships with the city, nonprofit organizations, and businesses, it is developing opportunities for participation, apprenticeships, internships, and jobs.

### Opportunities for participation

In Chicago, as in many other cities, a broad range of organizations provides opportunities for participation, including small grassroots programs; local free-standing organizations; affiliates of national youth-serving organizations like Boys and Girls Clubs and Ys; and civic organizations and faith-based groups, serving both young people and adults.[5]

After School Matters is adding to and integrating with the mix of opportunities for participation in a number of ways. Initially, it is increasing opportunities for participation in sports and physical fitness through its Club37 programs that operate through drop-in centers located at public schools and parks. Teenagers can join anytime and participate as often and in as many activities as interest them. Club37 offers activities as diverse as rowing, double-dutch jump rope, martial arts, hip-hop aerobics, sports leagues, and career-related sports and fitness field trips. Over time, ASM will expand opportunities for participation in activities in addition to sports.

### Apprenticeships

After School Matters is expanding apprenticeship opportunities in the arts, sports, technology, and communications, each with a hands-on community component. Apprenticeships operate in ten-week cycles. Instructors are recruited through a request for proposal process to work with groups of twenty youth. For example, Sports37 sponsors two apprenticeship programs. In the Lifeguard Apprenticeship, participants build swimming and water safety skills needed for certification as lifeguards. In the Sports Apprenticeship, participants learn skills as coaches and referees in five sports, with a focus on how to work with younger children. As another example, Words37 is designed to build literacy skills. Apprentices work with professionals who make their living with words, including storytellers, journalists, authors, performers, and poets. Apprentices develop reading, writing, and presentation skills by writing and showcasing stories at elementary schools, community-based organizations, and park districts and by helping to facilitate youth book clubs.

In its apprenticeship programs, ASM is developing a model of what apprenticeship opportunities for adolescents should look like, the principles and practices on which they operate, and the financial and other administrative inputs they require.

### Internships and employment

After School Matters has developed summer internships for youth who have participated in its apprenticeship programs. In the summer of 2002, Sports37 apprentices were employed as lifeguards at the Chicago Park District's beaches and pools and in their day camps. The Park District and community organizations hired apprentices as sports and recreation counselors. Words37 apprentices worked at museums, Head Start centers, and public health facilities as storytellers and docents.

The City of Chicago is also creating pathway opportunities for youth internships and jobs. In response to cuts in federal funding, the Mayor's Summer Youth Program began providing internships in 2001 for fourteen and fifteen year olds and part- and full-time jobs for young adults sixteen to twenty-one years old.

Internships are structured as learning opportunities, providing introductions to the workplace as well as stipends. Youth who spend a summer as interns are eligible for paid employment the following summer. During the eight-week summer break, public agencies, nonprofit organizations, and companies offer full- and part-time jobs, enabling summer school students to work in the afternoon.

The Mayor's Summer Youth Program hires college students and other young adults with work experience as account executives. They help recruit and work with corporations and then interview and match youth applicants with particular interests and experience to companies with specific skill and experience needs. They also act as liaisons between youth and corporations to help mentor youth and resolve problems.

### Creating access to information and opportunities

As part of the citywide infrastructure they are creating, ASM and the City of Chicago are partnering to develop an accessible, comprehensive inventory of opportunities for children and youth. This inventory and on-line Web site (www.ChicagoKidStart.org) contains information on resources for infants through adolescents that can be searched by postal code, cost, and times when they are available. This information can also be accessed by calling 311, the city's nonemergency information line. In addition, the Chicago Department of Human Services funds YouthNets, community agencies that provide local coordination, planning, and referral for out-of-school time opportunities.[6]

As part of the KidStart Web site, the City of Chicago, ASM, the Chicago Public Schools, and corporate partners are developing an on-line youth portfolio designed to acknowledge youth learning, skill building, and contributions. With active on-line coaching, teenagers will be guided in creating a record of their in- and out-of-school experiences and the knowledge, skills, and personal qualities they have developed and demonstrated.

The portfolio will enable youth to collect recommendations written by adults involved in these activities; record information on honors, awards, certificates, or licenses they have earned; and hold examples of their original work in text, audio, video, and graphic formats. These examples will include PowerPoint presentations, J-PEG and mp3 copies of art, music, and other original work, links to Web sites they have designed, and video clips of their performances.

Youth will be able to draw on information in their portfolios to apply on-line for out-of-school opportunities, including internships and paid employment, and to submit applications for postsecondary training programs, college admission, and financial aid. High school students in the Chicago Public Schools will be introduced to and use the portfolio as part of their school classes, but any youth will be able to create and update their portfolio on the KidStart Web site.[7]

## Opportunities and challenges

Creating a system of out-of-school opportunities capable of operating at scale faces critical hurdles. They include the absence of sufficient opportunities for young people, particularly in low-income neighborhoods, and the need to improve the quality of what exists; the lack of adequate, reliable funding; and the need to mobilize a broad political and civic constituency invested in the lives of young people in the out-of-school hours.

Acknowledging the learning and skill building that occurs for youth and crediting or compensating them for their growing skills and contributions are additional challenges that require attention. Both of these challenges are related to reinforcing the learning that occurs in out-of-school settings, and both are critical to the financing and civic action needed to generate and sustain a system of this kind.

### Acknowledging out-of-school learning

For youth, the knowledge and skills they gain in out-of-school settings can be as important as in-school academics. And recognition of these competencies can matter to youth, particularly if it helps them access opportunities that interest them.

Certificates and licenses in such areas as technology and sports are ways of acknowledging youth skills. By and large, though, for adolescents, the products, performances, and other tangible results of youth initiative in the out-of-school hours are evidence of competencies they have gained. Performance or portfolio assessment conducted in the midst of hands-on activities may be the kinds of assessment most aligned with the goals of promoting youth engagement and demonstrated achievement.

If done well, documenting knowledge and skills gained by youth is a way of holding adults working with them accountable for the quality of their own contributions and performance. Demonstrating youth competencies is also a way to reinforce the investment of organizations—government agencies, businesses, and others—in creating next-step opportunities for youth. Given the results orientation among policymakers and funders, it is unlikely that they will make and maintain the commitments needed to expand and sustain out-of-school opportunities for adolescents without evidence of their benefits.

A critical quandary is how to demonstrate learning benefits without undermining the engagement of both youth participants and adult instructors. It is crucial that out-of-school opportunities avoid the incentives of teaching to the test present in high-stakes, standards-based school reform and the testing associated with it.

### Credit and other forms of compensation

As youth participate in activities in the out-of-school hours that parallel required or elective school courses and as they demonstrate the competencies they are gaining, it begs the question of whether schools should—or why they should not—grant credit for them.

Providing credit for participation and learning in out-of-school opportunities can leverage the resources and expertise of organizations that focus on subjects that schools expect youth to master and can supplement the schools' responsibility for both mandating and providing them. As important, it recognizes the reality that youth learn across the settings in their lives.

In fact, through ASM and elsewhere in the country, examples exist of places where students are receiving credit for out-of-school learning. Credit is provided for elective courses and, less frequently, for core academic subjects. The following are examples based in Chicago and elsewhere:

Participants in Words37 have received community service credit for literacy activities with children in elementary schools and community organizations.

The Manchester Craftsmen's Guild and the Pittsburgh Public Schools have created the Arts Collaborative, an arts-centered program run at and by the guild. The program for ninth-grade students integrates the arts with mathematics, social studies, science, and English and is part of students' accredited work.

At Gallery 37's downtown Center for the Arts high school, juniors and seniors earn advanced placement credit for arts classes conducted daily from 2:00 P.M. to 4:00 P.M. The Chicago Public Schools has appointed an on-site principal who oversees these classes.

In Providence, Rhode Island, the Metropolitan Regional Career and Technical Center (popularly known as the Met) is a public high school where students are involved in applied learning internships across a variety of public, nonprofit, and business settings. Driven by student interests, these internships constitute the bulk of student academic learning. Credits are based on competencies demonstrated at student presentations.

These examples reflect an appreciation for learning that occurs in the out-of-school hours, which Heath and McLaughlin describe as "the best of both worlds."[8] For some time, they and other researchers and policymakers have promoted recognizing the learning that occurs in and out of school.

In addition to credit, forms of compensation in the nonschool hours include stipends for apprenticeships and internships and wages for youth employment. Compensation matters to adolescents as evidence of their increasing independence and as access to the rewards of work. In surveys conducted by Chapin Hall Center for Children at the University of Chicago, 48 percent of apprentices say that they participate in ASM to learn new skills and 45 percent to earn money.

However, there are inherent concerns associated with compensation. One is the risk of tipping the motivation for participation from implicit to explicit rewards. Pathways to the future need to

offer authentic activities that attract and retain adolescents independent of the credit or other compensation they provide. Relying
on pay should not erode the quality of these opportunities or their
intrinsic value to youth. In addition, compensating youth through
stipends and wages is costly. ASM and the City of Chicago are
faced with raising significant funding and engaging the public, nonprofit, and business sectors in providing internship and employment opportunities for youth, both tough to do, particularly in
tight economic times.

Creating a system of pathway opportunities for youth involves
several sequentially related and reinforcing steps: ensuring that
there are sufficient high-quality opportunities for youth, increasing access to and participation of young people in them, demonstrating the learning and other benefits that occur, and reinforcing
the civic commitment and financial support needed to sustain these
opportunities over time. This system is portrayed in Figure 4.2.

The assumptions embedded in developing this system are that
creating engaging, accessible out-of-school opportunities will
increase youth participation in them. In turn, participation over time
will extend the interest that initially spurs young people to participate and will increase their engagement, mastery, and other positive
outcomes. Documenting these outcomes will reinforce the civic
commitment and financial support needed to sustain this system.

Chapin Hall is working with ASM to develop a program of
research focusing on the availability and use of out-of-school
opportunities in Chicago and the effects of youth participation in
them. It will incorporate a specific focus on the programs provided
and youth outcomes demonstrated by ASM and will take a broader
look at the availability, distribution, use, and effects of out-of-
school program participation on youth in a diverse set of Chicago
neighborhoods.

This research will provide critical information to inform the
planning and implementation of ASM and other organizations providing youth opportunities. It will also provide essential information on their effectiveness. Like authenticating youth competencies
gained through participation, evidence of positive benefits from

# Figure 4.2. A system of pathway opportunities for adolescents

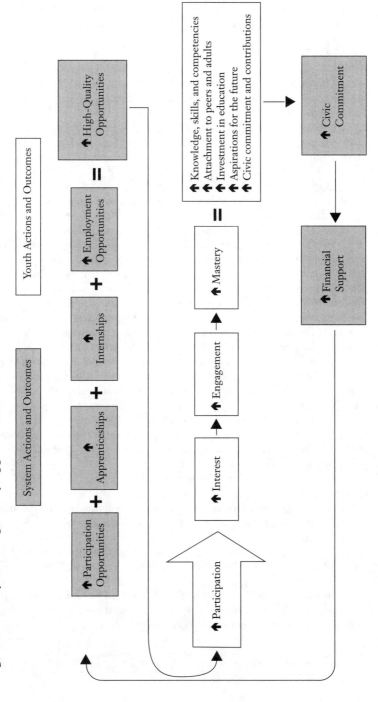

System Actions and Outcomes

Youth Actions and Outcomes

Participation Opportunities + Apprenticeships + Internships + Employment Opportunities = High-Quality Opportunities

Interest → Engagement → Mastery

Participation

- Knowledge, skills, and competencies
- Attachment to peers and adults
- Investment in education
- Aspirations for the future
- Civic commitment and contributions

Civic Commitment

Financial Support

rigorous research can reinforce civic interest and financial investment in creating a system of pathway opportunities for youth.

## Notes

1. This evidence includes the fact that for youth on their own, the after-
school hours are the period with the highest incidence of destructive behavior to themselves and others. Centers for Disease Control and Prevention.
(2001). *Youth Risk Behavior Surveillance System.* Available on-line: http//
www.cdc.gov/nccdphp/dash/yrsb/index.html. Adolescents are also subject to
the recently identified negative effects of welfare reform. Gennetian, L., Dun-
can, G., Knox, V., Vargas, W., Clark-Kauffman, E., & London, A. (2002).
*How welfare and work policies for parents affect adolescents: A synthesis of research.*
New York: Manpower Research and Demonstration Corporation.

2. Csikszentmihalyi, M., & Schneider, B. (2000). *Becoming adult: How
teenagers prepare for the world of work.* New York: Basic Books.

3. Mortimer, J. T., & Johnson, M. K. (1998). Adolescents' part-time work
and educational achievement. In K. Borman & B. Schneider (Eds.), *The adolescent years: Social influences and educational challenges.* Chicago: University of
Chicago Press.

4. In 1997, Gallery 37 received an Innovations in American Government
award sponsored by the Ford Foundation and Harvard University's Kennedy
School of Government. It has inspired programs in fifteen U.S. cities, as well
as in London and Birmingham, England, and Adelaide, Australia.

5. The City Department of Human Services, through its Youth Services
Division, is one of the largest funders of out-of-school programs in Chicago,
supporting programs for both children and youth. R. Ogletree, T. Bell, and
N. Smith described the role of the Chicago Department of Human Services
and the alignment of its initiatives and others in Chicago in Ogletree, R., Bell,
T., & Smith, N. K. (2002). Positive youth development initiatives in Chicago.
In G. G. Noam & B. Miller (Ed.), *Youth development and after-school time: A
tale of many cities.* San Francisco: Jossey-Bass.

6. For a discussion of the Youth Services Division and YouthNets, see
Ogletree et al. (2002).

7. While low-income youth typically have more limited access to computers than their more affluent peers do, it is worth noting that of the thirty-seven
thousand completed applications received for the 2002 Mayor's Summer
Youth Program, more than twenty thousand were submitted over the Internet, and just over 70 percent of these applicants reported receiving free or
reduced-price school lunch.

8. Heath, S. B., & McLaughlin, M. W. (1994). The best of both worlds:
Connecting schools and community youth organizations for all-day, all-year
learning. *Educational Administration Quarterly, 30*(3), 297.

JOAN R. WYNN *is a research fellow at the Chapin Hall Center for Children at the University of Chicago.*

*Free-choice learning, a new paradigm for the learning that youth and their families engage in outside school, can play an important role in the healthy development of youth, their families, and communities.*

# 5

# Optimizing out-of-school time: The role of free-choice learning

*Lynn D. Dierking, John H. Falk*

*Lynn D. Dierking, John H. Falk*

ON A RECENT spring Saturday, Rawanda Collins, an eleven-year-old girl from Dayton, Ohio, woke up early, too excited to sleep.[1] This morning, she, her grandmother, and her cousin Tashika were going to participate in a Girls at the Center (GAC) program at the local science museum. GAC is a collaborative effort between the Franklin Institute Science Museum in Philadelphia and the Girl Scouts of the U.S.A., with financial support from the National Science Foundation. The program provides science experiences for girls and an adult partner (a parent, guardian, or other significant adult) in economically disadvantaged communities across the country. Participants attend a series of Discovery Days at the local museum or science center on a particular topic such as "Electricity" or "Water" and also enjoy a full day of other activities, such as attending an IMAX film and having free time to explore. At the culminating Family ScienceFest event, girls and their adult partners share their science experiences with friends and family members.

NEW DIRECTIONS FOR YOUTH DEVELOPMENT, NO. 97, SPRING 2003 © WILEY PERIODICALS, INC.

Although many of these programs are free, participation requires a commitment. For example, GAC events in Dayton were held Saturday mornings, a difficult time for Rawanda and Tashika's grandmother because she worked the night shift and usually did not get any sleep before bringing the girls to the events. However, she had never seen them so excited about science before, and they seemed to be learning a great deal, so she wanted to support that learning. And an adult component of the program emphasized the importance of children's learning inside and outside school, shared gender data about how girls were often not encouraged enough in science, and explained that most girls lacked the necessary preparation to pursue science careers if they chose. This too made her eager to attend. And truth be known, she also enjoyed herself; it was fun doing the activities together and spending quality time with her grandchildren. . . . She was also learning things about science she had never known before!

Rawanda, Tashika, and their families are only a few of the hundreds of thousands of children and youth and their families across the country who have participated in structured learning opportunities such as GAC; the GAC project alone has served thousands of girls since its inception in 1996. In addition to these types of programs specifically targeted at disadvantaged communities, millions of school-aged children in virtually every community in America participate annually in organized sports programs, arts and crafts and dance and drama classes, as well as summer camps, computer camps, and a huge assortment of other extracurricular activities. These are more than mere enrichment experiences. For example, through the GAC program, thousands of girls have learned about life sciences, physics, chemistry, and the environment.

These efforts provide youth with some of their most fundamental and important educational lessons, exposing them to new activities, helping develop their skills in relevant contexts, supporting long-term, meaningful relationships with adults, and fostering collaborative learning experiences that facilitate their transition from childhood to adulthood. Interestingly, these lessons are learned not because they have to be, but because the participants choose to learn them. This learning is not limited to a single institution in a single city; it occurs every day at hundreds of similar institutions in virtually every community in the United States. What is this phenomenon?

## Free-choice learning

Learning is something we do all the time throughout our lives, in school and at home, in classrooms, in workplaces, through cultural activities, while watching television, playing sports and talking with friends.[2] What we learn depends on what we already know and understand, whom we are with, where and when we learn, and, importantly, why we are motivated to learn in the first place. Sometimes we learn through formal instruction and sometimes on our own. Some of what we learn, we learn because we have to. However, much of what we learn we learn because we want to, because events in our lives intrinsically motivate us to find out more.[3] Under these conditions, we learn not only what we want, but also where, when, and with whom we want. This is free-choice learning, learning that is guided by learners' needs and interests—the learning that people engage in throughout their lives to find out more about what is useful, compelling, or just plain interesting to them. This type of learning is intrinsically motivated and largely under the choice and control of the learner. Surfing the Internet, participating in book discussion groups, watching nature documentaries on television, checking out books at the library, and visiting museums and parks with friends and family are all examples of free-choice learning.

As the United States continues its transition from an industrial society to an information society, learning across the life span is increasingly important, and free-choice learning is an essential component. Youth and their families are spending increasing amounts of time engaged in such learning—at home, after work, and on weekends.[4] The free-choice learning sector of television, radio, the Internet, museums, magazines, newspapers, books, parks, and community organizations of all types—youth, religious, environmental, health, sports and recreation, and a complex interpersonal network of families, friends, and acquaintances—is part of a vast educational infrastructure that helps to support the ongoing and continuous learning of American youth and their families.[5] Sadly, this sector is underrecognized and seriously underfunded despite the fact that it provides more educational opportunities to more people, more of the time, than schooling or workplace learning combined. The free-choice learning sector is also the most diverse, fastest growing, and arguably the most innovative of these sectors, and it can play an important role in support of youth development.

## The out-of-school landscape

In order to optimize free-choice learning opportunities for youth, we need to understand the landscape within which youth spend their daily time daily time is spent. The Forum for Youth Investment has developed a conceptual framework that visually breaks down learning opportunities for youth by time and by place, suggesting that learning happens during the school day and outside the school day, inside school and out in the community (see Figure 5.1). Intended as a conceptual rather than a representational model, this framework dramatically demonstrates opportunities for free-choice learning, a significant component of at least half of the spaces in the model. Interestingly, it also points out some of the problems with current approaches to young people's development, for although a huge amount of time, money, and effort flows into supporting and improving one of these quadrants, the school day inside the school, relatively little was invested in the other three-quarters of the model until recently.

This relative lack of investment is potentially problematic in the light of the educational value of youth's out-of-school time; in addition, this model actually overestimates the time youth spend in

**Figure 5.1. Where and when learning occurs**

Where Learning Occurs

|  |  | In the School Building | In the Community |
|---|---|---|---|
| **When Learning Occurs** | During the School Day | School classrooms and other school spaces | Libraries, museums, colleges, businesses |
|  | Out of School | School buildings, community schools | Families, community-based organizations, faith community, parks and recreation, community centers |

school. The current model implies that school day learning is divided evenly between the classroom and the community. Yet well over 98 percent of all youth spend well over 98 percent of their school days within the four walls of the school.[6] Although field trips, community service projects, and work-study and internship opportunities exist and are known to be effective learning tools, they rarely involve many children for many hours of the day.

The four-square framework also suggests that youth spend equal amounts of time inside and outside school. Current estimates by the U.S. Department of Education, however, suggest that children spend in excess of 90 percent of their waking hours outside the classroom.[7] Even the recent "explosion" of before- and after-school programming does not influence this situation greatly; although a growing movement, the majority of youth in the United States are not enrolled in such structured programs (by 1999, an estimated 6 million children K–8 were participating in before- and after-school programs and an estimated 8 million to as many as 15 million "latchkey children" on any given day go home to an empty house after school).[8] And even when youth do participate in programs housed in school buildings, they are frequently administered and implemented by autonomous youth development organizations and therefore are intermediary environments more appropriately labeled "community" in this model.[9] Figure 5.2 shows the modified model reflecting actual time use data. We believe this more precise representation of youth's out-of-school time draws attention to the vital role that free-choice learning plays in youth development, yet society consistently undervalues this type of learning.

It is our belief that as a society, we fail to recognize and value the learning that occurs outside credentialed institutions. Because free-choice learning is underappreciated, it is also underfunded, diluting its presence and impact. Federal support for free-choice educational institutions, such as libraries, museums, community-based organizations, national parks, and public television and radio,

**Figure 5.2. A more realistic breakdown of where and when learning occurs**

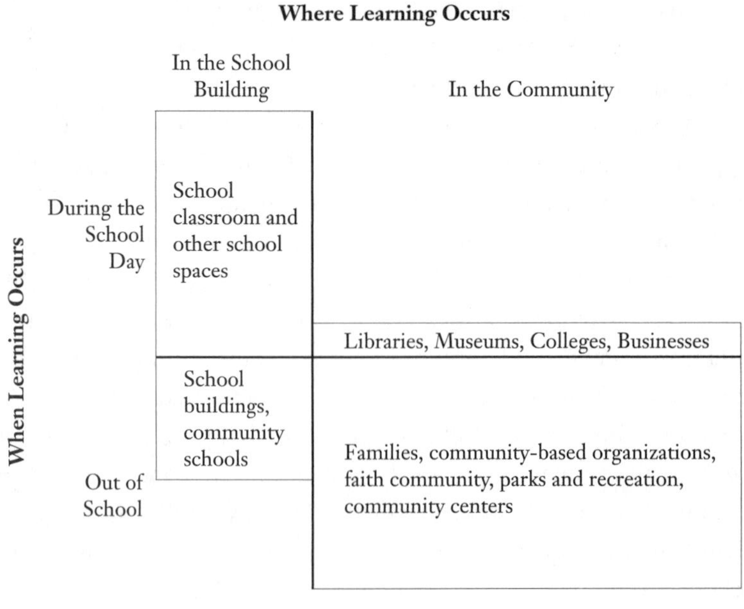

represents roughly 1 percent of the nation's total expenditures on public education.[10] And unlike the 99 percent of public education funding exclusively earmarked for the 40 to 50 million youth in schools, this 1 percent supports all 270 million American citizens, not just youth.

In addition to these challenges, it has been difficult to document systematically and meaningfully the learning that does occur in free-choice settings (settings in which the learner has significant choice and control over the learning that occurs). If youth do spend more than 90 percent of their time outside school, do they actually learn anything of value during that time? Our research, and that of others, would suggest that the answer is an unequivocal yes.

First, as emphasized by the Forum for Youth Investment, there is a wealth of learning needs, beyond academics, that is essential to healthy youth development. These needs include a range of nonacademic cognitive skills such as knowing how to pay bills, cook dinner, and take care of an automobile. There are also important social and emotional competencies, as well as moral, physical, civic, social, cultural, and vocational capabilities. Equally, if not more, important are the skills of knowing how to learn and stay informed throughout one's lifetime. Currently, the primary focus of schooling is on reading and math, and unfortunately in many situations, instruction still revolves around rote computation and memorization or other mindless activity. Basic literacy and numeracy skills are necessary for success in the twenty-first century but not sufficient.

Free-choice learning is an untapped resource that represents a significant percentage of all academic and nonacademic learning in the United States. Through free-choice learning, youth can acquire and develop an understanding of a wide array of subjects, learn basic life skills such as how to collaborate on projects and communicate with others, and develop a sense of leadership and responsibility. Free-choice learning can also yield significant learning in cognitive areas normally considered exclusively school subjects.

## Public understanding of science

For nearly half a century, science education has been an educational priority in the United States. Billions of dollars have been poured into schools at every level to strengthen the quantity and quality of science education. Nevertheless, on national tests of science knowledge, Americans of all ages fare poorly. Among adults, only those who have had college-level courses in science do well.[11] We believe that these studies underestimate public understanding of science because they focus on general school-based science learning as measured by multiple-choice exams. Our sense is that public understanding in science is far more situation specific: a deeper understanding of a few selected areas of personal interest rather than generalized knowledge of the entire domain of science as measured by such tests. We have worked over the past twenty-five years to advocate and document the benefits of such free-choice learning, and this work is beginning to yield important data. We offer findings from two studies that demonstrate the importance of free-choice science learning.

In 1997, the Institute for Learning Innovation launched an investigation to help determine how, when, where, and why people learn science.[12] This study focused on adults, but its lessons are applicable to youth also. A random telephone survey of Los Angeles residents ($n = 1,002$) was conducted as one aspect of the investigation. The sample of adults (over eighteen years of age) was broadly representative of the Los Angeles community and closely mirrored U.S. Census data for the community in terms of age, race, ethnicity, household income, educational attainment, and gender.[13]

People interviewed were asked to rate their interest in science on a scale from 1 to 10, with 1 indicating very low interest and 10 very high interest. The median response was 7.0 (mode = 10, S.D. = 2.6); nearly half indicated a scale score of 8 or higher, regardless of age, race, ethnicity, income, education, or gender. Similarly, when people were asked to rate their knowledge of science, they overwhelmingly rated it as average or slightly higher than average. On the surface, it appeared that the public's self-perception of their science knowledge was somewhat inflated, but like any other self-report data, such ratings are relative. The question is on what basis the public was reporting their knowledge. If knowledge was based on a national normative test such as these previously cited, the results would seem discrepant. But there could be an alternative explanation.

Our suspicion was that the discrepancy had to do with the nature of the questions asked and the methods used to answer them in national science literacy investigations. Every U.S. citizen probably did know quite a bit about science, but rather than the knowledge of a survey course in science, their knowledge varied widely and was very topic specific, and practical.

To test this hypothesis, we conducted a second round of random telephone interviews ($n$ = 877) and asked everyone to describe some area of science in which they felt they knew more than the average person.[14] Virtually everyone we talked to felt that there was at least one area of science that they had some reasonable knowledge of and that exceeded the norm. Some people described very specific areas of scientific knowledge; others gave more general categories, such as health or the environment. We validated people's claims of knowledge by asking them to give some examples of their understanding. With only a few exceptions, self-reported knowledge was credible.

Sources of the public's knowledge of science varied. Roughly a third of the people claimed to have learned their favored science topic primarily in school, just under a quarter said they acquired their knowledge on the job, and the largest number, nearly half of all those surveyed, claimed to have learned science during their leisure time, through some kind of free-choice learning experience. People described learning science by using the Internet; reading magazines and books; going to museums, zoos, and aquariums; and participating in special-interest clubs and groups. These findings are consistent with data collected by others, demonstrating widespread use of free-choice learning resources for acquiring science information.[15]

The recently completed five-year longitudinal study of 324 participants of G.A.C., the program described at the outset of this chapter, provides additional evidence for the impact of free-choice

learning experiences.[16] Findings suggested that the program provided valuable and much-needed opportunities for girls and adults
to engage in positive free-choice science learning experiences, not
opportunities that all participating families traditionally engaged in.
Participants responded very favorably to a major strategy of the program: immersing girls and adults in the activities of doing science,
that is, observing, classifying, experimenting, and hypothesizing.

Participating girls also found these free-choice learning experiences
personally meaningful. Paralleling other studies, many of the girls
distinguished what they called "GAC science" from "school science,"
noting that they used to think science was boring and hard, especially
in school. These same girls seemed to love GAC science, suggesting
that it is "fun because you get to build and create things and you don't
have to memorize lots of stuff that does not really make sense [to you
personally]." Findings also suggested that participating in GAC was
not only improving girls' self-reported interest in and attitudes toward
science, but also beginning to influence their perceptions of themselves as scientists, as well as their ability to recognize connections
between science and everyday life. Girls' self-confidence and perceived efficacy in science improved to the point that after participating in more than one GAC event, the number of girls contemplating
science-related careers rose from 13 percent to 53 percent.

The program also positively influenced adults who had participated. They were much more aware of the importance of science
learning for girls and how to support and facilitate their science learning, inside and outside school. These outcomes persist over time as
well. Findings from a series of recent retrospective investigations at
the Children's Museum of Indianapolis focused on the Great Scientific Adventure Series and Y-Press, two in-depth programs for pread-
olescents and adolescents, suggested that these two programs had
lasting and meaningful impacts on participants (some impacts per-
sisting as long as six years), facilitating learning across four broad
dimensions: changes in perspective and awareness, social development, interests, and knowledge and skills.[17] The programs not only
influenced individual growth but also had a marked effect on family
dynamics and development and long-lasting impact on adolescents'
connections and contributions to their community. These outcomes

are clearly ones that any society would hope any quality education program, inside or outside school, could facilitate.

## Creating seamless learning experiences

A vibrant free-choice learning sector is as fundamental to youth development as are quality schools, a thriving economy, and healthy, safe communities. To successfully educate youth today, the U.S. education system cannot be based solely on schooling; it must also include a focus on free-choice and workplace learning. In fact, there is growing evidence that the more the three educational sectors of school, work, and free-choice learning overlap seamlessly in youth's lives, the more likely they are to become successful lifelong learners.[18] Each of the three components—formal schooling, the workplace, and free-choice learning sectors—needs to be engaged and working together toward common goals. Currently, all three are functioning largely in isolation, each driven by widely differing perceptions of what their educational goals and role in society should be. In our opinion, achieving this goal requires equal and complementary support for the learning that occurs inside and outside school, within the school building and in the community and workplace. This means seeking additional funding for free-choice learning efforts and youth experiences outside school that supplement the educational outcomes typically associated with schooling.

An important first step toward creating seamless learning opportunities would be to identify the essential learning goals for each sector during each stage of life that would together form an integrated, holistic system for lifelong learning. We recently identified the following free-choice learning goals for older children and youth, designed to complement the goals of schooling and workplace learning for that age group:[19]

1. To develop and practice lifelong learning skills in real-world contexts
2. To engage in more in-depth study of topics or areas of interest than schooling experiences generally offer

3. To learn and interact with family and other significant adults in increasingly meaningful ways, modeling adult thinking and social problem solving including acceptance, self-confidence, self-monitoring, and team play
4. To explore and experiment with efforts to be increasingly independent and responsible
5. To begin to master skills and interests, make initial decisions about the kind of life they hope to pursue and build, and in the process develop a sense of self
6. To find supportive mentors, particularly peers and adults other than parents, who can provide guidance and supervision as youth practice and experiment with lifelong learning skills

The development of goals for each of the educational sectors is just one of many tasks that lie ahead in the effort to create seamless lifelong learning opportunities for youth. There is considerable evidence that school-initiated learning experiences occurring outside school have tremendous benefits, and workplace learning experiences have also been linked with increasing engagement in learning, reducing dropout rates and increasing the likelihood of college enrollment.[20]

There is good news and bad news as we move forward. The good news is that the key constituents for change are already in place; the United States possesses one of the finest learning infrastructures (schooling, free choice, and workplace) in the world. The bad news is that the infrastructure lacks coherence and leadership. Change requires undoing deeply ingrained beliefs and habits and must be a grassroots effort, with vision and leadership from the top. This task is not as insurmountable as it might seem. Although these changes require time, careful thought, and much restructuring, the raw material, the know-how, and certainly the need and desire exist. What we have lacked is a comprehensive vision of learning, a vision we hope that this chapter has begun to elucidate. We need the leadership and the will to make change happen.

In the meantime, here are some specific recommendations that could be implemented sooner rather than later and would in our opinion significantly speed the change process:

- Focus educational reform efforts on individuals rather than institutions. Make the lifelong learning success of each youth the focus of educational policy, regardless of age, income, race, ethnicity, gender, or religion.
- Restructure all departments of education at the national, state, and local levels into departments of learning to encompass all types and degrees of lifelong learning in the schooling sector, but also the free-choice learning and workplace sectors.
- Ensure that federal, state, and local support for education is more equitably distributed to all parts of the educational infrastructure. The free-choice learning and workplace learning sectors deserve and require as much attention and financial support as the formal schooling sector.
- Create a lifelong learning budget for every citizen, and provide structures to enable each individual to invest that budget wisely and carefully at any time in their lives and within any part of the educational infrastructure.

### Notes

1. Rawanda Collins and Tashika are pseudonyms.
2. Falk, J., & Dierking, L. (2002). *Lessons without limit: How free-choice learning is transforming education.* Walnut Creek, CA: AltaMira Press.
3. McCombs, B. L. (1991). Motivation and lifelong learning. *Educational Psychologist, 26*(2), 117–127.
4. Falk & Dierking (2002).
5. We use the term *sector* here to refer to organizations whose business it is to support public learning and education outside school.
6. Institute on Education and the Economy. (2001). *School-to-work: Making a difference in education.* New York: Teachers College, Columbia University.
7. Metz, M. (2001). The 9 percent challenge: Education in school and society. *Teachers College Record.* Available on-line: http://www.tcrecord.org/Content.
8. Miller, B. (2000, June). Update of the National Child Survey of 1990. National Institute on Out-of-School Time; Seppanen, P., Kaplan, de Vries, D., & Seligson, M. (1993). *National Study for Before- and After-School Programs.* Washington, DC: Office of Policy and Planning, U.S. Department of Education; National Center for Education Statistics. (1999, Spring). National Household Education Survey.
9. Noam, G. G., Miller, B. M., & Barry, S. (2002). In G. Noam & B. Miller (Eds.), *Youth development and after-school time: Policy and programming in large cities.* New Directions for Youth Development, no. 94. San Francisco: Jossey-Bass.

10. Lewenstein, B. V. (2001). Who produces science information for the public? In J. H. Falk (ed.), *Free-choice science education: How we learn science outside of school* (pp. 21–43). New York: Teachers College Press.

11. Miller, J. D. (1998). The measurement of civic scientific literacy. *Public Understanding of Science, 7,* 1–21; Miller, J. D. (2001). The acquisition and retention of scientific information by American adults. In Falk, pp. 93–114; Miller, J., & Pifer, L. (1996). Science and technology: The public's attitudes and the public's understanding. In National Science Board (Ed.), *Science and engineering indicators: 1996* (pp. 7.1–7.21). Washington, DC: U.S. Government Printing Office. Falk (2001).

12. Falk, J. H., Brooks, P., & Amin, R. (2001). Investigating the role of free-choice science learning on public understanding of science: The California Science Center L.A.S.E.R. Project. In Falk, pp. 93–114.

13. National Science Board. (1998). *Science and engineering indicators: 1998.* Washington, DC: U.S. Government Printing Office.

14. Falk, J. H., & Coulson, D. (2000). *Preliminary analysis of second telephone survey: California Science Center L.A.S.E.R. Project* (Tech. Rep.). Annapolis, MD: Institute for Learning Innovation.

15. National Science Board. (1998). *Science and engineering indicators: 1998.* Washington, DC: U.S. Government Printing Office; Korpan, C. A., Bisanz, G. L., Boehme, C., & Lynch, M. A. (1997). What did you learn outside of school today? Using structured interviews to document home and community activities related to science and technology. *Science Education, 81,* 651–662.

16. Adelman, L., Dierking, L. D., & Adams, M. (2000). *Summative evaluation year 4: Findings for Girls at the Center* (Tech. Rep.). Annapolis, MD: Institute for Learning Innovation.

17. Luke, J., Cohen Jones, M., Wadman, M., Dierking, L. D., & Falk, J. H. (2002). *Phase II Programs study: The Children's Museum of Indianapolis* (Tech. Rep.). Annapolis, MD: Institute for Learning Innovation.

18. Hacker, R., & Harris, M. (1992). Adult learning of science for scientific literacy: Some theoretical and methodological perspectives. *Studies in the Education of Adults, 24,* 217–224; Medrich, E. A. (1991). *Young adolescents and discretionary time use: The nature of life outside of school.* Paper commissioned by the Carnegie Council on Adolescent Development for its Task Force on Youth Development and Community Programs.

19. Falk & Dierking (2002), pp. 76 & 92.

20. Institute on Education and the Economy (2001).

LYNN D. DIERKING *is associate director of the Institute for Learning Innovation in Annapolis, Maryland.*

JOHN H. FALK *is director and founder of the Institute for Learning Innovation in Annapolis, Maryland.*

*The Worcester, Massachusetts, district-community plan for reinventing high schools shows how learning can be enhanced and transformed through intentional connections to community.*

# 6

# Blurring boundaries: The promise and challenge of a district-community action plan for systemic high school change in Worcester, Massachusetts

*Thomas Del Prete, Laurie Ross*

CHANGES IN today's society and economy require that public schools make transformations in education practices, policies, and learning environments. Urban school systems face additional challenges due to the socioeconomic situation of their students and families, high rates of mobility, and racial, ethnic, and linguistic diversity. The primary mission of public schools is to educate children. Given the broad range of students' needs and levels of readiness to learn, however, urban schools cannot be expected to provide the crisis intervention, risky-behavior prevention, and youth development supports that all students need to be effective learners. It takes collaboration across a broad range of community partners to meet this full variety of youth needs.

Young people are more engaged when they see connections between classroom learning and community life. They benefit from exposure to a wide range of adult roles. They need meaningful

NEW DIRECTIONS FOR YOUTH DEVELOPMENT, NO. 97, SPRING 2003 © WILEY PERIODICALS, INC.

opportunities beyond the limits of the school day—after school, on the weekends, and during the summer. Community organizations provide the contexts and resources for student support, learning, and development. When community organizations and schools work in partnership—when urban areas create seamless school-community learning environments—students and families benefit in measurable and immeasurable ways.

The Forum for Youth Investment has put forth a vision for young people's learning that blurs the lines between school and community learning environments and the hours during which young people engage in meaningful learning activities (see Chapter One, this volume). The Forum argues that learning opportunities must be of high quality, readily available where and when young people need them, and creating developmentally appropriate ladders of opportunity across a K-12 continuum. To realize this vision of continuous learning opportunity for all young people, communities must address what the Forum calls the bottom-line issues: resource development, public engagement and demand, accountability, leadership, and vision.

In this chapter, we discuss the Carnegie Corporation of New York's funded Schools for a New Society Initiative in Worcester, Massachusetts. We outline the five core components of the district-community plan for reinventing high schools, briefly summarize the planning process that led to their development, and discuss aspects of the collaborative effort that illustrate how bottom-line issues are being addressed in Worcester. We pay particular attention to some of the tensions inherent in blurring school-community boundaries to achieve systemic high school change.

## Worcester's approach to the Carnegie challenge

In the spring of 2000, the Carnegie Corporation invited Clark University's Jacob Hiatt Center for Urban Education and the Worcester Public Schools, along with a number of similar partnership groups in the country, to develop a district-community plan for the systemic reform of urban high schools. The invitation marked the beginning of a multiyear effort to develop a system of high schools effective in ensuring high achievement among all students of all backgrounds. In stipulating the need for a combined district-community endeavor, Carnegie was harnessing the idea that fundamental change would require points of leverage from within and outside schools and that broad-based collaboration and commitment were essential.

## A rationale for Worcester's participation in the Carnegie initiative

Worcester was a good candidate for the Carnegie initiative because of the challenges it faces and the potential for a coordinated large-scale effort to meet them. Although the city is comparatively small, with a population shy of 175,000 and including approximately 26,000 public school students, Worcester has struggled to close the achievement gap that separates the poor from the middle class, and minority students from their white counterparts. Although income correlates with performance more than any other factor in Worcester, as it does elsewhere, the city's fast-growing Latino student population, close to 28 percent of the overall student body, is affected most dramatically. Recently, over 80 percent of the city's Latino high school students did not pass the high-stakes statewide test on their first try.

There were many signs that the combined district-community effort to transform high schools that Carnegie envisioned would develop in Worcester. Among the most notable were pockets of partnership activity in the city. The Worcester Pipeline Collaborative, for instance, had linked the University of Massachusetts Medical School and North High School in a common effort to support academic work, scientific literacy, and career awareness in the health sciences. Clark University, in particular through the Hiatt Center for Urban Education, had developed a strong professional development collaborative that encompasses teacher preparation, ongoing professional learning, and education reform.

The university was also deeply involved in a neighborhood renewal project at the center of which is a new middle/high school, University Park Campus School (UPCS), serving a diverse, economically poor population.[1] UPCS promises a tuition-free education at Clark for every student who qualifies. Although only in its fourth year at the time of the Carnegie invitation, UPSC was already emerging as a model of small school effectiveness.

### Core goals and tensions

In the spring of 2000, the Worcester Education Partnership (WEP) was formed in response to the Carnegie challenge. The fledgling WEP included representatives from higher education institutions, ethnic constituencies, youth service agencies, and cultural institutions, in addition to the school district. Earning a planning grant from Carnegie, the WEP embarked on a year-long process of rethinking the idea of high school. This process was oriented in part by an emphasis on reenvisioning school-community relationships that support student achievement and youth development. We aimed to reconceptualize the learning environment based on fundamental ideas about youth development, about what students need to grow personally and academically, and the intimate relationship between these two. We were striving to foster a seamless environment for growth, encompassing both in-school and out-of-school experiences.

Five main themes frame the vision of effective high schools that resulted from this process:

Small, personalized learning communities—developing small learning communities that unite clear expectations for academic achievement, a unified curriculum philosophy, personalized peer and adult support (teams, clusters, academies, and small schools), community provision of academic resources, and community involvement in school governance

Academic opportunity, support, challenge, growth, and achievement—integrating literacy, numeracy, and academic learning across the curriculum; building academic competence; providing opportunity for inquiry-driven and interdisciplinary, team-

based projects; basing learning on proficiency and mastery of
standards rather than time; and combining rigor and relevance
(that is, connecting curriculum and community life)

A collaborative professional culture—developing learning communities based on collegiality, reflection, inquiry, and a commitment
to develop collaboratively content expertise and best practice

Youth development—developing active roles and support for young
people in every aspect of school and community life

School-community integration and partnership—developing strategies to expand and sustain a broad base of parental support and
involvement; building awareness, support, and partnerships
among key constituencies and the community in general; working with area colleges in developing small schools and other partnerships; developing a coordinated school-community effort to
promote youth development

Among the most important goals of the planned actions is an
increase in the achievement of minority and low-income students
across the district, outside current pockets of effectiveness.

It has proven challenging to implement this vision in Worcester,
as in the other Carnegie-supported sites.[2] Blurring boundaries necessarily means rubbing up against them; sometimes it is only in
pushing on them that they are uncovered. Some boundaries have
deep generational and historical roots. The process of change has
meant establishing more bilateral communication and dialogue
within and between traditionally hierarchical structures. It has
involved a joint effort that redefines responsibilities for student
achievement and development, working toward a new distributive
and collaborative leadership model. Perhaps most difficult of all, it
has meant trying to transcend the politics of authority and control—the visible and invisible boundaries set up by individual
schools, the district, community agencies, and constituency groups
that must be blurred in order to move from a collection of dis-
jointed efforts to a single collaborative one. However apparent the
potential benefits for youth and the community, and in spite of
the commitment of key stakeholders and leaders, the path between

action plan and actual practice is full of switchbacks, backtracks, and uncertainties.

---

## The bottom-line issues

The bottom-line issues put forward by the Forum for Youth Investment—related to demand, resources, accountability, and leadership—correspond closely to the various ways in which WEP has been seeking to integrate school and community. In Worcester's school redesign efforts, joint school-community efforts have driven efforts to secure demand and public will, marshal and align available resources to support young people's learning and development, build accountability both inside and outside the schools, and secure the leadership necessary to support significant change in school structure and instruction.

### Demand: Constituency engagement

Family involvement and community engagement were key areas of joint district-community planning within the WEP. The goal was to develop a conceptual framework and corresponding set of "best practices" strategies to strengthen the home-school alliance for students. Representatives from the district, community, and university formed a family involvement planning committee. As the planning year progressed, the need for a parallel process of engaging, organizing, and mobilizing ethnic community stakeholders became increasingly clear.[3] One concern was to understand the gaps in achievement from the perspective of these communities and, in the process, develop their awareness, collective voice, and capacity to respond constructively and proactively. A more fundamental issue involved the perceived and real distance between the lives of poor and ethnic minority students and school experience.

Four basic aims emerged to shape the engagement process:

- To provide out-of-school support for students and families, ranging from guidance in navigating the school landscape to academic tutoring and adult mentoring

- To enhance the openness, communication, and relationship between schools and families from these communities
- To build mutual support for student achievement and mutual understanding of what support is effective
- To establish awareness of differential school performance; to elicit recommendations, responses, and support with respect to the more personalized and collaborative school models developing in the planning process; and to plan for community representation in governance councils at the school level

Together these aims reflect the need for communities sufficiently organized to address critical issues, the need for a collaborative structure among these communities and between the communities and schools to ensure good communication and mutual problem solving, and the need for an organized role in accountability and governance.

The internal organization of the three main ethnic groups and the creation of a coordinated overarching group represents one of the most substantial developments of Worcester's school reform efforts. The example and pace have been set by the Latino community, organized as the Worcester Working Coalition for Latino Students, with the Latino Education Institute at Worcester State College as its institutional arm. Guided by determined leadership and with an advisory board of community leaders, the Latino coalition was emerging as a united force at about the same time that the WEP was gaining momentum in the high school planning process.

The African American community group, called Uniting Our Voices, and the Southeast Asian group, called the Southeast Asian Coalition of Central Massachusetts, are both on the path of organization building. At the same time, all three are supported by each other within the framework of the WEP, in particular by the family–community involvement coordinator housed at the Hiatt Center for Urban Education. Together with Worcester Community Connections, a group supporting the poor and underserved, they have formed UCALA (United Caucasian, Asian, Latino, African-Americans). UCALA has helped new small schools to organize parent meetings that are responsive to the needs of diverse families. UCALA will also support a teacher recruitment effort with the Hiatt Center and district to diversify the teaching force.[4]

These developments are important and necessary to the process of change, but there remain tensions and ongoing needs. There is an ongoing question of how to integrate the voices and support of these communities into the school reinvention process. Internally, implementing plans for dramatic changes in structure, professional and organizational culture, curriculum, teaching, and assessment is very challenging for school leaders and teachers. Mutual trust is a central theme in this internal process, as it is in the process of community collaboration. School personnel have to learn to trust that the presence and participation of community members will be beneficial, and not add time and undue stress, as much as community members will need to learn to have trust in them.

### Resources: Accessing and aligning community resources

During the planning phase of this process, we frequently reflected on the idea that although additional, secure resources are always needed, Worcester did in fact have many programs and resources in the schools and community. The main problem was that these resources lacked adequate coordination and alignment. The WEP saw two types of community resources—those that aim to support youth development broadly and those that can be tapped and integrated in teaching the core academic curriculum—as particularly critical aspects of the reform effort.

*Youth development.* Rather than being treated as a separate change area, youth development was a theme that ran through all aspects of the school-community planning process. Therefore, the School-Community Youth Development Partnership Subcommittee's charge was to explore systems and culture change options to support young people—rather than introduce new programs into the district. The committee worked to develop a structure that would expand the current pockets of excellence to cover all young people and during all of the times young people need services— during school, after school, on weekends, and during the summer. Expanded responsibility for youth well-being would alleviate some of the burden on the schools and make teaching and learning easier and more satisfying for all.

Consisting of local leaders in the fields of youth development, business, health, and education, this subcommittee used youth development and child resiliency frameworks to create a plan that builds on the strengths of the WPS and the city's community organizations. It identified three key outcomes of the plan:

- Schools and community organizations will coordinate, strengthen, and unify their relationships, services, and vision for youth.
- Families, teachers, staff at community-based organizations, and mentors will be better equipped to support student learning and achievement.
- Youth will lead, participate in, and make important decisions in and out of school to increase their engagement and ownership over their education and the other parts of their lives.

Over the course of six months, the committee designed a coordinated school-community youth development model to ensure equity and equivalency in service and resources delivery and organizing and coordinating systems (see Figure 6.1). The model, described in Table 6.1, integrates various levels of the school district with many segments of the community and incorporates existing school-community relationships where possible.

In this model, a district-level community resource facilitator will identify, coordinate, monitor, and evaluate the community resources. This facilitator will establish quadrant-level interagency committees and task forces to ensure that each quadrant of the school district has access to programs, resources, and services corresponding to the five youth development competency areas. Each student would have a Student Success Plan created by a school-community liaison working with the facilitator and the small school or team. Small school teachers, community-based organization staff, parents, and the young person would have significant input in the creation, implementation, and assessment of the plan. Plans would include student academic, health, artistic, career, civic,

**Figure 6.1. School-community integration model for Worcester, Massachusetts**

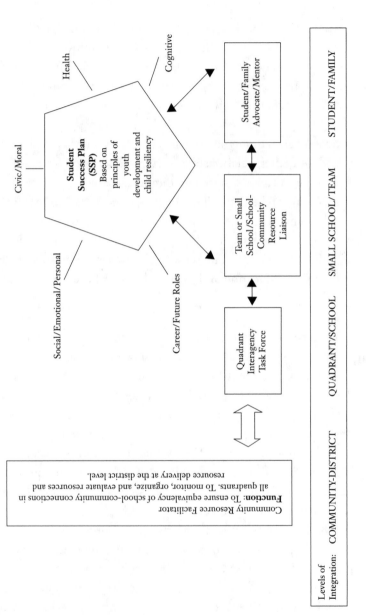

## Table 6.1. Description and framework of the school-community integration model, Worcester, Massachusetts

| Plan Component | Purpose |
|---|---|
| Oversight organization | ▶ Ensures equivalency of school-community connections and resources in all quadrants<br><br>▶ Monitors, organizes, and evaluates resources and resource delivery at the district level<br><br>▶ Attracts new resources and forges new connections with community organizations |
| Quadrant-based interagency task forces | ▶ Streamlines processes to integrate school and community services, programs, and resources<br><br>▶ Organizes services at the small school or team level<br><br>▶ Technology (using, for example, on-line resource inventories and virtual meetings) facilitates the functioning of the interagency task forces |
| School-community resource liaison | ▶ Creates a Student Success Plan (SSP) for each student in the small school or team. This person's connection to the interagency task force will ensure that he or she brings knowledge of the full range of community supports to the plans. The small scale of the team or the small school will ensure that the liaison knows each student well enough to develop a meaningful plan. |
| Student Success Plan based on youth development and resiliency | ▶ Allows significant input from students and families in determining how students will achieve their educational and future goals<br><br>▶ Requires that each student experience a balance between school and community learning opportunities<br><br>▶ Coordinates plan assessment in the school and community. Technology—specifically online SSPs—can facilitate plan implementation, monitoring, and assessment. |
| Student-family advocate— The mentor | ▶ Ensures that the SSP is implemented as the student, family, and other team members designed it |

personal, social, and other current needs and would link future aspirations and goals with a variety of extracurricular activities and supports. Students would have increased responsibility over the pace and the means by which to complete the plan.

Although there is commitment to the principles laid out in the plan, the implementation of the school-community integrated model has not been the partnership's top priority in the first year. Much effort has gone into designing new small schools, recruiting students, professional development, and renegotiating school-district relationships. This model also requires a new way of thinking about youth. Teachers and other school staff need to see themselves as youth development workers, just as traditional community-based youth workers need to see themselves as teachers. Furthermore, this model shifts the youth-adult relationship to one of partnership and shared responsibility for student education. Partnership requires a deep level of trust and rapport between young people and the adults who work with them.

*Curriculum boundaries.* The boundaries between school and community are often bridged through curriculum. Workplace internships and community service opportunities are familiar and important in the high school curriculum in Worcester, as they are elsewhere. In our planning, however, we set a broader goal. Believing that engagement would increase if academic tasks were connected to students' community life, we sought to make the community both a subject of and a place for the curriculum by bringing the curriculum to the community and the community to the schools. At the same time, we shared Carnegie's commitment to prepare students for active participation in forming and sustaining multicultural democracies.

The WEP's Community Curriculum Committee, with representation from cultural and scientific organizations in the city, redefined and developed several curricular partnerships with the schools. Community partners kept in mind the overall goals of the initiative in areas such as literacy, the development of academic competencies consistent with state curriculum standards, and engagement with community resources and the world of adult work. A plan designed by the Worcester Center for Crafts and the Higgins Armory Museum focusing on medieval life was piloted in ninth-grade history and English language arts classrooms. The high school literacy-across-the-curriculum initiative, which, among other practices, engages students in literary discussion through book clubs, has begun, on a very limited basis, to involve out-of-school programs supported by community groups as well as an in-school effort. Other plans, such as an interdisciplinary urban ecology curriculum that would combine hands-on scientific investigations in the community with historical and literary study, are waiting in the wings.

Several factors complicate the effort to activate community-based curriculum plans. Although they have been developed to align with state curriculum standards, the plans do not slide easily into the curriculum units developed by teachers to meet state and district requirements. Moreover, the intensity of converting large high schools into small schools and of establishing new literacy development practices makes the addition of new curriculum difficult. Our hope is that new partnerships between each small school and different community agencies will facilitate the adoption of school-community curriculum models over time.

### Leadership: Transformations in school-based governance

Governance and accountability are closely intertwined. In creating a governance structure for Worcester's effort, the key challenge was to create a group that would ensure the formal representation of community voices, address constructively the issues involved in implementing the district-community action plan, and advise the district leadership and core partner accordingly.

The WEP steering committee, comprising community leaders, the superintendent, and the project director, meets monthly to discuss progress and issues. Over time, it will examine data and reports produced through the evaluation process. Members also will visit with school-based leaders to talk through issues and progress at that critical level.

At the school level, newly formed governance boards will mirror the purpose of the WEP steering committee on a large scale. We expect that teachers and leaders from each small school will join with UCALA representatives and core community partners on these boards to inform program and policy development, advise on the development of the annual school improvement plan, and analyze student performance and participation data. The boards in this respect will expand on the role of school councils already mandated by Massachusetts law.

### Accountability: Monitoring and tracking structures

When blurring the line between school and community, it is essential to have two loci of accountability: community based, meaning groups that are not bound to the old way of doing things and are freer to demand change, and internal, meaning those school-community partners most directly responsible for designing and implementing change and for monitoring, implementing, and evaluating outcomes. Although both forms are important at all phases, the community-based lever of accountability in Worcester proved to be crucial during the planning phase (prior to the establishment of the partnership steering committee). Worcester's Working Coalition for Latino Students played this role. The internal lever is gaining prominence during implementation in the form of an in-depth study of how students are experiencing the process of school change.

*Latino Coalition.* The Latino Coalition is helping to rearrange the boundaries between school and community by establishing both a strong independent voice and a voice for change within the WEP. This dual identity developed only after members of the coalition evaluated the goals of WEP planning and the prospects of having a real voice in the process. Leaders made clear that they would sign on fully only with the assurance that their concerns for more opportunity and support for Latino students would be heard and their advocacy role honored. Their organizational strength, bolstered by resources from the state legislature as well as grant-making foundations, has led to the establishment of programs, such as an after-school academic support program (ISLA, Innovative Services for Latino Adolescents), that directly support Latino students. They have hosted several public forums on Latino student performance on the statewide test and have held districtwide meetings on the benefits of small schools for all students.

*Worcester Education Partnership Cohort Study.* Ensuring that implementation remains true to plan design and assessing the effectiveness of Worcester's plan for deep and interconnected forms of classroom, school, district, and community changes requires a mixed-method, multilevel, and longitudinal research and evaluation plan. The use of participatory methods is also crucial to gain insight into how different stakeholder groups experience secondary school transformation and to involve students directly in data analysis and project implementation. The WEP Cohort Study meets these criteria. The main purpose of the study is to gain a deeper understanding of how students experience the process of school change and the impact of school change on their academic achievement, motivation, sense of themselves as learners, future aspirations, and relationships with teachers, students, and community members.

While school practice and student performance data will be tracked over five years at the district level, the cohort study is designed to follow a sample of students attending the new small schools in greater depth. Cohort students will be interviewed about their experiences as the school becomes more personalized. Surveys will be sent home to their families and to any community-based programs in which they participate. Focus groups will be conducted with a subgroup of the cohort each spring.

High school students will play several active roles in the evaluation activities. First, several students from each small school will be recruited as student researchers. These young people will document changes in student and teacher behaviors, attitudes, and practices. Second, student focus groups will not just be about extracting knowledge. Rather, these focus groups will be opportunities to share data with students for their analysis. This form of focus group will provide a rich context in which to understand quantitative indicator changes. Most important, as students become engaged in data review and analysis, they will be able to make informed recommendations about areas for additional change, and they will feel ownership over the recommendations. This will increase the likelihood that students will advocate for additional involvement in the school transformation process.

The combination of methods, including different types of new and evolving small schools (such as schools within schools, freestanding schools, and vocational, each with different themes and schedules), in conjunction with a sample stratified by academic performance, will allow us to examine how different types of school environments and practices benefit a wide variety of learners. Again, the key tension involved with this form of accountability is that the source—the voice of young people—is not the traditional location of school accountability.

## Conclusion

Our experience thus far affirms the importance of addressing bottom-line issues of vision, community demand and commitment, resources, leadership, and accountability in the formation of a district-community partnership working to establish a youth-centered learning environment across school-community boundaries. It suggests further the importance of cultivating and aligning various sources of leverage strategically in all aspects of planning, implementation, and evaluation, with young people themselves as part of the process. Finally, it suggests the importance of anticipating and responding to the different tensions that arise during both the planning and implementation phases. The challenge of cultural change is implicated throughout: the need for reculturing schools and communities as more collaborative entities with academic achievement and youth development as their guiding mission. Issues of trust, relationship, and communication are embedded in this process. For all of this complexity, our experience indicates that the possibility of a communitywide educational ecology that supports the development and achievement of all students is real.

### Notes

1. Over 75 percent of the students at UPCS qualify for the federal free or reduced-cost lunch program.

2. The other partnership sites are in Boston, Chattanooga, Houston, Providence, Sacramento, and San Diego.

3. The Latino, African American, and Asian American communities are key constituencies in Worcester, representing about 28 percent, 12 percent, and 8 percent, respectively, of the student population.

4. The Hiatt Center at Clark University was awarded a three-year federal Title II Teacher Recruitment grant in fall 2002 for this purpose.

THOMAS DEL PRETE *is director of the Hiatt Center for Urban Education at Clark University and project director of the Carnegie Schools for a New Society initiative in Worcester, Massachusetts.*

LAURIE ROSS *is the coordinator of the Community Development and Planning Program within the Department of International Development, Community and Environment at Clark University and is the local evaluator for the Worcester Education Partnership.*

*The community can serve as a resource to help students become more engaged in learning and strengthen connections between schools and community.*

# 7

# Community as text: Using the community as a resource for learning in community schools

*Martin J. Blank, Sheri DeBoe Johnson, Bela P. Shah*

LISTENING TO THE debate culminating in the No Child Left Behind Act of 2001 and following the act's early implementation, it would be easy to assume that the only things that matter in terms of improving student learning happen in the classroom. The role of family and community receive short shrift.

But researchers and practitioners agree with what every parent knows. Learning starts early. It happens at home and in neighborhoods, as well as at school—wherever young people with curious minds spend time. And because young people learn in so many different ways, it happens best when it is encouraged and connected across all three settings. In schools that provide high-quality teaching and a wide array of experiences and skill-building opportunities in a variety of community environments, learning is deepened and strengthened.[1]

We address these issues through the Coalition of Community Schools, an alliance of education, youth development, family

NEW DIRECTIONS FOR YOUTH DEVELOPMENT, NO. 97, SPRING 2003 © WILEY PERIODICALS, INC.

support, health and social services, community development, phil-
anthropic, and governmental organizations that serves as a united
voice for creating different and better public schools—community
schools. The coalition envisions a community school as a place and
a set of partnerships where an integrated focus on academics, services, supports, and opportunities leads to improved student learning, stronger schools, and healthier families and communities.

## *What is a community school?*

Community schools are open to students, families, and community
members before, during, and after school and throughout the year.
Before- and after-school programs build on classroom experiences
and help students expand their horizons, contribute to their communities, and have fun. Family support centers help with parent
involvement, child rearing, employment, housing, and other services.
Health and social services are available. Parents and community residents participate in adult education and job training programs and
use the school as a place for community problem solving.

Community schools use the community as a resource to engage
students in learning and service and help them become problem
solvers and asset builders in their communities. Volunteers come to
community schools to support young people's academic, interpersonal, and career success. Families, students, principals, teachers,
neighborhood residents, and leaders from community agencies and
institutions decide together how to support student learning. Their
collaboration strengthens families and builds healthier communities.[2]

The capacity to do more of what is needed to ensure young people's success, and to do it effectively, makes community schools
both different and better. By linking school and community
resources, community schools do three things that schools, acting
alone, cannot:[3]

- Provide additional resources and a variety of learning opportunities so that all the conditions for learning that are critical for
  student success are in place.

- Focus on developing both academic and nonacademic competencies, a combination that improves long-range learning outcomes.
- Build social capital by connecting students with their neighbors and community networks and the school and the community.

## Creating the conditions for learning in community schools

The conditions for learning are rooted in research from numerous disciplines and practice areas, including early childhood and adolescent development, education, family support and family studies, health and social services, and community development. Community schools have the ability to fulfill all of the following conditions for learning, fostering a learning environment in which every child can do his or her best:[4]

Condition 1: A core instructional program with high standards and high expectations for students, qualified teachers, and challenging curriculum provides for academic excellence.

Condition 2: Students are motivated and engaged in learning in both school and community settings and during and after school.

Condition 3: The basic mental, physical, and emotional health needs of young people and their families are addressed.

Condition 4: There is mutual respect and effective collaboration between families and school staff.

Condition 5: Community engagement, together with school efforts, promotes a school climate that is safe, supportive, and respectful and connects students to a broader learning community outside the school.

We focus here on how using the community as an integral part of the school curriculum—what we have come to call community as text—helps students become motivated and engaged in learning (Condition 2) and builds strong connections between the school and community (Condition 5). The community-as-text approach uses the history, culture, challenges, and circumstances of the community as the content for learning, rather than just the information provided in textbooks.

The focus on community as text for curriculum is particularly important because it connects the work of the community explicitly to the primary mission of the school: improving student learning. It also helps students apply what they are learning at school to their daily lives, strengthens students' sense of connection to their community, and enables students to experience the value of contribution. Community is not just involved with student learning in the nonschool hours. It is a resource for learning during the school day. Given the narrow focus on accountability and testing, we are deeply concerned that this promising approach is being crowded out of children's educational experience.

## Common characteristics of community-as-text approaches

Although there are several community-as-text models, our analysis suggests that they share common characteristics:

• A focus on real family and community conditions and challenges. Every community has its own history, culture, environment, and challenges, and every family has its own culture and experience. Community-as-text curricula use these realities as the content of curriculum.

• Reinforcement and extension of standards-based reform. Standards provide a framework for curriculum development and student assessment. Curriculum connected to community and daily living is designed to reflect these standards. It does so in a manner that helps students improve their reading, language, and math skills and enables students to reach standards related to civic involvement and education.

• Student engagement and motivation. Schools and communities should have high expectations for all students. Challenging learning experiences that focus on the real problems of communities where young people live help them become active learners. At the same time, this kind of curricular approach provides necessary support and structure so that each student feels valued and is encouraged to develop latent talents.

• Student involvement in program development, implementation, and evaluation. When young people are given a greater responsibility in their own learning process, student motivation increases, student discipline improves, and teacher effectiveness grows. Schools are microcosms of society. When schools involve students appropriately in curriculum development, they ". . . mirror the democratic values they seek to instill . . . so that every child's participation, regardless of ability (and background), is needed and wanted."[5]

• Young people as resources to their communities. Adults typically see young people through the narrow, and too often negative, perspective of the media. When the community is used as text, young people can become assets in their community, helping to solve specific problems alongside peers and adults.

• Collaboration between schools and organizations and individuals in the community. All community partners—youth, parents, concerned citizens, youth development organizations, social service providers, community-based organizations, businesses, religious institutions, local government, institutions of higher education, and others—have a vested interest in the education and welfare of their youth. These partners, often with a deeper understanding of community history, culture, and dynamics, can support curriculum design and implementation by providing schools and youth access to a broader array of community resources. Collaborative decision making between school and community partners helps to deepen the school's relationship to the community.

## Community-as-text models

We draw on four different models to describe the community-as-text approach: service-learning, academically based community service, environment as an integrating context for learning, and place-based education. The concept of community as text also is embedded in related areas of work, such as democratic schooling, civic education, civic engagement, and school-to-work programs, among others that we cannot address here.

### Service-learning

Service-learning is a "teaching method through which citizenship, academic subjects, skills and values are taught. It involves active learning, drawing lessons from the experience of performing service work."[6] Service-learning takes place in K-12 schools, higher education classrooms, and community-based organizations. The service itself should address a genuine community need and be thoughtfully organized to help in solving a community problem. In quality service-learning programs, the service project meets both a real community need and classroom goals. This allows students to improve academic skills and apply what they learn in school to the broader community.

Service-learning at Nicholas Senn High School in Chicago, for example, has clearly had a positive impact on the school climate. When Senn adopted a service-learning program in 1997, its administrators, teachers, staff, and students were working hard to get the school off academic probation and raise low test scores and attendance. Five years later, probation is a thing of the past. Reading and math scores have risen, attendance rates have increased, disciplinary issues have declined, and attitudes toward school have improved.

Many teachers at Senn are committed to integrating service-learning in their curriculum. One Spanish teacher, for example, not only teaches her students how to speak Spanish but also uses service to relay the importance of understanding other cultures, developing good family relationships, and caring for people of all ages. The students adopt *abuelos*, or grandparents, at a day program attended by Hispanic senior citizens. This year-long commitment gives the students an opportunity to practice their Spanish while developing relationships with seniors, many of whom lack any family support.

Teachers at Senn use service-learning to make what they are teaching relevant to real life.[7] When a history teacher lectured on the issue of hunger in America, the students researched and discussed the topic and what they could do to help the problem. Representatives from a local food bank visited the classroom to discuss their day-to-day challenges. The students then volunteered at the food bank, packaging three tons of food in one day. In all, more than a thousand students from all grade levels have been involved and have donated more than thirty-seven thousand hours of service.

Research indicates that service-learning builds citizenship, increases students' sense of responsibility and workplace skills, and reduces negative behavior. Service-learning experiences also are associated with academic achievement gains among students in elementary, middle, and high school; foster greater engagement in schoolwork and increase problem-solving skills; and increase student attendance.[8]

### Academically based community service

Academically based community service, as developed by the Center for Community Partnerships at the University of Pennsylvania, provides hands-on real-world problem-solving experience. It builds serious and sustained engagement that transforms students in the university and in public schools into active citizens and community members. Senior faculty members have designed nearly a hundred courses focused on community revitalization for this purpose. Undergraduates work with teachers and students to develop curriculum and engage public school students as peer teachers or coresearchers.[9] These courses (examples are "Urban University-Community Relationships: Integrating Learning, Teaching, Research, and Service Through Action-Oriented, Real-World, Problem Solving," "Math Community Teaching Project," and "Strategies to Prevent Early Childhood and Adolescent Asthma") are implemented through a partnership between the university, the West Philadelphia Improvement Corporation, and neighborhood schools.

Academically based community service shares much with service-learning, but is distinguished in an important way: it involves the faculty and students of institutions of higher education, as part of their core teaching and learning mission, in partnerships with local school teachers and students. It reflects the efforts of a growing number of institutions of higher education to take responsibility for helping to improve the quality of life in the places where they are located.

The Urban Nutrition Initiative illustrates the academically based community service model. Francis Johnston, professor of anthropology at the University of Pennsylvania, redesigned his course on human growth and development to create the initiative with his students and Turner Middle School teachers. The focus of the course is now community health, with the aim of improving the nutrition and health of public school students, their families, and the local community. The initiative has developed and implemented a curriculum that teaches math, social studies, and language arts through entrepreneurial projects, alongside peer and community health promotion. Specific projects include student-run school community gardens and a produce stand, a fitness program for parents and community members, and urban agriculture and microbusiness development. Positive results from this initiative include lower consumption of nonnutritious snack foods on the day following the opening of the school produce stand and increases in the consumption of fruit and vegetables by 70 percent and 200 percent, respectively. The level of community participation in fitness activities also increased.

Turner students who have moved on to high school formed the Youth Driven Service Learning Center to promote civic engagement and academically based community problem solving. Recently, the youth developed a Web site through which young people express their opinions about environmental health and nutrition issues. In addition, these students have partnered with University of Pennsylvania students to explore the development of a neighborhood food cooperative and health resource center.[10]

*Place-based education*

"The aim of place-based education is to ground learning in local phenomena and students' lived experience."[11] It can take a wide range of forms, each adapted to the unique characteristics of particular places, helping to overcome the disconnection between schools, students, and the communities where they live. Students and teachers use community concerns as the foundation for curriculum. Students are more actively involved in the creation of the curriculum, as well as the creation of knowledge, resulting in greater ownership and engagement. Teachers in these settings act as guides, co-learners, and brokers of community resources. Place-based education relies heavily on strong connections between school and community members.

An example shows a focus on family and community history and culture in a border town in Texas. Home to farmers and migrant workers of Mexican descent, the border town of Edcouch, Texas, is one of the poorest communities in the country. An estimated 40 percent of Edcouch-Elsa High School students move with their families to find work and have to leave school at midyear. In the face of massive turnover, a new approach to teaching students and families about their community conceived by the Llano Grande Center for Research and Development has led to strong feelings of loyalty and connection, causing young people to return and make Edcouch their home.

Llano Grande began by having students and teachers collect stories from family, friends, and elders. Students transcribed their interviews, translating and editing them into narratives for publication in English and Spanish. K-12 teachers now weave parts of these oral histories into their own curriculum to bring a "real" element to literature, music, art, journalism, media production, drama, and history. Children at all grade levels have reworked these stories into fiction, artistic depictions, and even a television documentary that Edcouch-Elsa High School students produced for the local PBS station.

Llano Grande's place-based education approach has improved morale, motivation, and instructional methods to create a greater sense of community-school connectedness. Together, these factors have contributed to improved performance on statewide Texas achievement tests. Sixty students have been accepted by the nation's top colleges and universities, and about thirty-six have attended or are attending Ivy League colleges, a symbol for this community of what their students can accomplish.[12]

### Environment as an integrating context for learning

Environment as an integrating context for learning (EIC) offers a framework for interdisciplinary, collaborative, student-centered, hands-on, and engaged learning. It uses natural and sociocultural environments as the context for learning, often through problem solving and project-based activities. EIC-based learning is not primarily focused on learning about the environment or limited to developing environmental awareness. It is about using a school's surroundings and community as a framework within which students can construct their own learning, guided by teachers using proven educational practices. Through team teaching, EIC helps to break down traditional boundaries between disciplines. Led by the State Education and Environmental Roundtable (SEER), EIC operates in partnerships with sixteen state education agencies (www.seer.org).

Hollywood Elementary School, located in Saint Mary's County, Maryland, a small farmland region bordering the Chesapeake Bay, uses this approach by focusing on recycling and the environment. In the late 1980s, after several failed attempts by citizens to start a community recycling program, the fifth-grade class at Hollywood decided to take on this issue, quickly turning their campus into a neighborhood recycling center. The school's hallways contained boxes of newspapers, and the school's parking lot became a regular Saturday morning stop for residents to dump their cans and glass. Parents volunteered to haul the items collected to the nearest recycling station in a neighboring county. Eventually, the county government set up a few recycling stations and hired a recycling coordinator.

Since that time, construction of a new school has opened up more hands-on learning opportunities. Students have turned their campus into a living lab that includes a nature trail, a butterfly garden, a forest habitat for migrating birds, and the transformation of a drainage pond into a natural wetland. In 1997, this approach helped fourth graders to perform 27 percent higher on the Maryland State Performance Assessment Program than other schools in the county and 43 percent higher than the Maryland state average.[13]

Confirming these results, an evaluation of EIC in forty schools by SEER showed improvements in reading, writing, math, science, and social studies; discipline and classroom management; engagement and enthusiasm for learning; and pride and ownership in community. Students using the EIC model scored higher than other students on 72 percent of the California academic assessments that measured skills in language arts, math, science, and social studies.[14]

## An action agenda for community as text

Enough is known about the effectiveness of community-as-text strategies to warrant an intensive effort to broaden and deepen its use during school as well as out of school, by schools and youth development organizations. Here are a few suggestions:

• Build a consensus on the purpose and principles of community as text. If community is to become an integral part of curriculum in public schools and not be seen as a special add-on project, leaders and advocates of different models must come together to articulate a common purpose and set of principles. Such a framework, teamed with existing research, can be used at the state and local levels to help educators and community leaders understand the value of the approach.

• Invest in more research. The research data presented here demonstrate the promise of the community-as-text approach to improving student learning and preparation for democratic life. Public and private funders will have to invest substantially greater resources in research that captures specific outcomes of this approach for students, schools, and communities to convince more policymakers and administrators of its potential.

• Develop a local community-as-text strategy. School and community leaders can connect different actors in the community pursuing community-as-text strategies. They need to look beyond people involved with the models discussed here to include an array of educators and community groups helping to create community-based learning experiences and enhance civic education and engagement. They should define common principles, review and disseminate research, and develop a plan to incorporate these approaches more explicitly in the school curriculum. Professional development opportunities for teachers also will be an important part of this strategy.

• Review community-as-text programs in states. We encourage state education agencies to look at various programs they fund or operate that fall within the broad concept of community as text. State leadership can help focus schools on how the community-as-text approach can help students achieve state standards.

• Incorporate community as text in administrator preparation. Few administrator preparation programs devote much time to the role of community in the education of our children. If community as text is to take root, these programs must devote time to helping prospective administrators understand the basics of how community works and the role of school in community.

• Include community as text in teacher preparation programs. The critique suggested for administrator preparation applies equally to teachers. Since community-as-text approaches bridge the curriculum and the community, they provide an excellent vehicle through which schools of education can help teachers understand how community contributes to student learning and help teachers develop and implement curriculum that uses the community as a resource for learning.

## *Conclusion*

Over two thousand years ago, Plato wrote that the most important task of educators is to teach young people to "find pleasure in the right things." Not so surprising, educators, particularly those working in schools that perform poorly and are pressured to narrow teaching strategies and subject matter to make sure that all students pass the test, have found it difficult to help students accomplish this goal. Consequently, the opportunity to realize the connection between student success and a range of other goals—helping young people develop interests, becoming actively engaged, strengthening their community, or developing high expectations for themselves—is lost.

Many community schools, however, have embraced Plato's vision for learning and have adopted community-as-text strategies. In these schools, young people experience the pleasure of doing something that has purpose to them; participating in learning activities that require skill, concentration, and involvement; and contributing to the quality of life of their community.

## Notes

1. Council of Chief State School Officers and Forum for Youth Investment. (2001). *Students continually learning: A report of presentations, student voices and state actions.* Washington, DC: Forum for Youth Investment.

2. Harkavy, I., & Blank, M. (2002, Apr. 17). Community schools: A vision of learning that goes beyond testing. *Education Week, 52.* Available on-line: www.edweek.org.

3. For more explanation on what makes a community school different and better, see Melaville, A., Shah, B. P., & Blank, M. J. (forthcoming). *Making the difference: Research and practice in community schools.* Washington, DC: Coalition for Community Schools.

4. For more on supporting research for the conditions for learning, see Melaville, Shah, & Blank (forthcoming).

5. Rural School and Community. (n.d.). "Capacity Building. Available on-line: www.ruraledu.org.

6. Learn and Serve. (n.d.). Available on-line: http://www.learnandserve. org/about/service_learning.html.

7. Learning in Deed. (2002). *Learning in deed: The power of service-learning for American schools.* Available on-line: www.learningindeed.org.

8. Billig, S. H. (1999). *The impacts of service learning on youth, schools and communities: Research on K-12 school-based service learning, 1990–99* [research summary]. Learning in Deed; Weiler, D., LaGoy, A., Crane, E., & Rovner, A. (1998). *An evaluation of K-12 service-learning in California: Phase II final report.* Emeryville, CA: RPP International and the Search Institute; Loesch-Griffin, D., Petrides, L. A., & Pratt, C. (1995). *A comprehensive study of project YES—rethinking classrooms and community: Service-learning as education reform.* San Francisco: East Bay Conservation Corps; Stephens, L. (1995). *The complete guide to learning through community service, grades K-9.* Needham Heights, MA: Allyn & Bacon; Follman, J. (1998, Aug.). *Florida Learn and Serve: 1996–97 outcomes and correlations with 1994–95 and 1995–96.* Tallahassee: Florida State University, Center for Civic Education and Service; O'Bannon, F. (1999). Service-learning benefits our schools. *State Education Leader, 17,* 3; Shaffer, B. (1993). *Service-learning: An academic methodology.* Stanford, CA: Stanford University Department of Education.

9. *Center for Community Partnerships at Penn.* (2001). Philadelphia: Center for Community Partnerships, University of Pennsylvania.

10. Johnston, F. E., Barg, F., Gerber, D., Rulf, J., & Harkavy, I. (in press). *Anthropology and the discipline gap: The Urban Nutrition Initiative as a model for*

*changing communities through educational reform.* Michigan Journal of Community Service Learning. Ann Arbor, MI.

11. Smith, G. A. (2002, Apr.). Place-based education: Learning to be where we are. *Phi Delta Kappan, 83*(8), 584–594.

12. See www.llanogrande.org. For other examples, see www.ruraledu.org.

13. Lieberman, G. A., & Hoody, L. L. (1998). *Closing the achievement gap: Using the environment as an integrating context for learning.* San Diego, CA: State Education and Environment Roundtable.

14. State Education and Environment Roundtable. (2000). *California Student Assessment Project: The effects of environment-based education on student achievement.* Available on-line: http://www.seer.org/pages/csap.pdf.

MARTIN J. BLANK *is the director of school, family, and community connections at the Institute for Educational Leadership and staff director for the Coalition for Community Schools, both in Washington, D.C.*

SHERI DEBOE JOHNSON *is partnership manager for the Coalition for Community Schools at the Institute for Educational Leadership in Washington, D.C.*

BELA P. SHAH *is program associate for the Coalition for Community Schools at the Institute for Educational Leadership in Washington, D.C.*

*A bridging typology captures a range of ways that after-school programs connect children's diverse worlds and support project-based learning.*

# 8

# Learning with excitement: Bridging school and after-school worlds and project-based learning

*Gil G. Noam*

IN NEW YORK CITY on a cool and sunny spring day in 2001, I visited an after-school program housed in an elementary school not far from the Museum of Natural History. The museum administers the after-school program, which is funded by The After-School Corporation (TASC).

The purpose of my visit was to witness the work our collaborative team (the Program in Afterschool Education and Research and Project Zero at Harvard University) had done to create project-based learning strategies in after-school programs. What I experienced there was quite remarkable. I saw a group of third and fourth graders as they were selling their cookies and crafts. They were excited that I was not as interested in their baked goods as I was in the colorful mosaics they had created on top of cigar boxes. The sale of each box provided them with $2.80. Who knows how they had arrived at that market value, but I did not care; they were so irresistibly enthusiastic that I immediately reached into my wallet.

In her excitement, the youngest of the three girls making the sale incorrectly subtracted from the three dollar bills I had given them

NEW DIRECTIONS FOR YOUTH DEVELOPMENT, NO. 97, SPRING 2003 © WILEY PERIODICALS, INC.

and was giving me back one of my three bills as well as twenty cents. But the older, more business-savvy, and maybe also more math-literate one quickly took back the change and correctly gave me two dimes. As I watched them in their shy yet amazingly successful experimentation with the entrepreneurial world (they had already moved on to the next customers), I decided to recreate with our team the steps they had gone through to reach their success.

These students had decided over many weeks of deliberation with two program staff members what their project would be. Together, the members of the group settled on a money-making venture because they were very troubled by the high incidence of cancer in their extended families. Almost all of them had lost a relative. They wanted to do something about this frightening illness and were going to donate their proceeds to the American Cancer Society. In order to make money, they were encouraged by the staff to work on a written business plan and a time line. After some refinement of the plan by the group, the children began their six-week creation of arts and crafts. What was compelling was not only their excitement and determination, but also the ways they critiqued and supported one another. The students also trained to add and subtract and, in general, to get their sales force ready for the week when they began selling to parents, other students, teachers, and administrators.

This young group of after-school students made more than three hundred dollars, and at a very touching occasion, the children handed an oversized check to an official of the American Cancer Society.

This is project-based learning at its best. Here, a group of after-school students democratically conceptualizes goals, learns how to write and revise a plan, works together to make creative products, and studies skills that enable them to perform the various tasks. Math is not just math anymore, but a way to get ready to sell. They worked through some of their sadness over losing loved ones by collectively doing something about it, thereby making the passively endured into an active pursuit. And these children reaped the benefits of reaching their goals, experiencing support from staff, teachers, and parents as they learned about generosity and organized giving.

Few would argue that this is impressive teaching and learning that fosters engagement, commitment, and community and skill building. This is also the type of learning that is going on in many after-school programs throughout the country. But it also a very time-consuming and difficult form of teaching, as we have learned in our work in New York City. This work requires a great deal of staff training and support and is the kind of teaching many school teachers shy away from because of the organizational complexities and coordination skills required. Ironically, some of the best pedagogy in after-school settings, typically accomplished with insufficiently trained staff, occurs far too rarely in schools with a trained workforce. And here lies an essential dilemma: although the informality of after-school settings lends itself to projects, community exploration, service-learning, and other participatory approaches to exploration and discovery and is fun, feels to children different from school, and allows them to develop their own voice, our research has shown us that after-school programs often lack the capacity to embark on this complex pedagogy.

Many after-school directors, youth workers, and policymakers worry about too much connection or integration with schools because they view schools as powerful institutions, even bureaucracies, that could easily overpower the structure and content of after-school time. Thus, a potential ally in learning, a reservoir of resources and know-how, often remains untapped. Projects such as the Cancer Society effort could become a bridge between the school day and the after-school program, even linked to curricular goals such as math, reading, and writing, and enriched through field trips, student decision making, and the integration of academic and nonacademic learning goals.

There is among many after-school leaders the hidden, and sometimes not-so-hidden, hope that innovative after-school pedagogy will eventually penetrate the schools. These leaders have as their goal not only to fill the out-of-school time productively, but to make the entire educational experience of children before, during, and after school better. Most after-school educators believe that after-school programs should feel, look, and be different from the school day but also that these programs should actively engage with schools and school personnel. Is there a way, many leaders ask, to connect the informality and small-group orientation of after-school programs with the more structured goals of the school day? How would one use, for example, projects across the school day and the after-school time? Could homework become more meaningful by integrating it into the projects initiated in the after-school hours?

The editors of this issue contribute greatly to this discussion through their spatial conceptualization of the different spheres of learning. They assembled chapters that show to what degree we need to stretch our notions of academic skills and success. These chapters showcase innovations from around the country that occur when schools and out-of-school programs are invigorated by community service, family involvement, and service-learning.

To make such ambitious goals a reality for many students everywhere, there has to be a productive organizational connection between schools and after-school programs, one that involves families and communities. Furthermore, there should be respectful interpersonal connections between teachers and after-school staff. And finally, there must be some knowledge of each group's educational goals. Is this one more educational utopia? Until recently yes, but there are now many experiments and models that can help shape the field of creative after-school education.

Bridging school and after-school does not mean that all programs must become school based or that they should become school-like. What is important is that programs aim to create some across-learning opportunities, achieve integration of some learning goals, and deepen children's exploration and skill acquisition, all the while respecting the existence of many types of learning that should be protected across a diversity of educational environments. Increasingly, after-school programs divide the time into nonacademic activities, such as sports and crafts, and academic activities, such as structured curricula or enrichment in language arts, science and math, and homework support.

In order to explore what some of the issues are that support bridging between schools and after-school settings, I conducted a research project together with Gina Biancarosa and Nadine

Dechaussay, two staff members of the Program in Afterschool Education and Research at Harvard University. We recognized, along with many others working in the field of after-school education, that without empirical evidence in the form of quantitative analyses, qualitative investigations, or even compendia of best practices, this emerging field of after-school education will make only marginal progress. We interviewed leaders in the field, visited many programs, and reviewed the existing literature to create a typology of learning and bridging. The model and findings are described in a recently released book, *Afterschool Education: Approaches to an Emerging Field*, as well as a forthcoming report of the Boston After-School for All Partnership.[1] What follows is a synopsis of our typology and implications for creative learning. I also explore the implications for project-based learning for each bridging type. Any project approach can exist within any type, but the nature of the mission, the academic and nonacademic goals, and the ideology around youth participation all combine to create different forms of projects.

## *Bridging*

Connecting children's diverse worlds in order to support learning, after-school programs act as "intermediary spaces."[2] Typically, these programs are produced by vibrant collaborations between different institutions and forces such as schools, families, community-based organizations and cultural institutions and university programs. Because after-school programs usually do not belong to any one constituency, they serve as a natural intermediary for children. After-school connects to academic work, but without serving as a school, and takes on aspects of family life (such as comfort, security, and recreation), but without becoming a family. To support children's learning requires more than a simple introduction of school goals and methods into the after-school context. What is needed is a concerted effort to connect children's divergent worlds so that their learning becomes more meaningful and relevant to their life experience.

In our own research and intervention studies, we have used the term *bridging adolescent worlds* to express the attempt to foster a sense of continuity for youth as they traverse their cultural contexts.[3] After-school programs, because of their informality, allow for in-depth and flexible adult-child relationships, can invite families and community to participate in programming, and have the ability to connect with schools. Thus, they have the potential to function as an essential environment, connecting the multiple worlds of children.[4]

## Bridging domains and types

In our initial efforts to understand bridging between schools and after-school programs, we were struck by the lack of theoretical conceptualization on the topic. For that reason, we began by simultaneously collecting data and developing a productive typology of bridging using Max Weber's approach to ideal typing. Our typology describes the intensity of bridging in programs and remains neutral to the question of what type of intensity is best. This is because the appropriate type of bridging depends on the mission and goals of each program.

Programs typically bridge within three domains: interpersonal, curricular, and systemic. These domains are not mutually exclusive but often co-occurring (see Figure 8.1). The most common domain

**Figure 8.1. Domains of bridging between school and after-school programs**

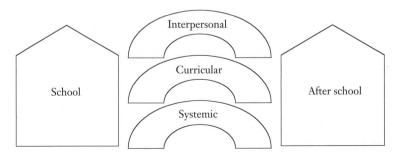

we found was interpersonal bridging, which ranges from serendipitous meetings between school and after-school staff to regular contact between school and after-school staff by telephone, e-mail, and other means. How productive the impact is also depends on whether the flow of information is reciprocal or one-way. In many of our interviews, after-school staff complained about the difficulty of establishing contact with busy school personnel.

Curricular bridging consists of attempted alignment between school and after-school curricula. Compared to interpersonal bridging, the positive impact of curricular bridging depends less on reciprocity and more on clear articulation of goals and consistent development of curricula that engage and challenge children.

Systemic bridging entails the sharing of governance, funding, transportation, and systems. For example, decision-making teams in both institutions might incorporate members from both institutions, ensuring a certain level of collaboration. The meetings of such teams could range in their sphere of influence from the needs of individual children to future directions for the school and program.

Considering both the domains and dimensions of bridging makes it possible to categorize programs according to the intensity of their relationships with schools. The following typology provides a scale of intensity from Self-Contained (programs and schools that do not interact interpersonally or organizationally) to Unified (programs and schools that have been brought together such that there is no distinction between the two institutions). Between these poles we distinguished three other types—Associated, Coordinated, and Integrated—with each representing a gradual increase in bridging intensity from one pole to the other (see Figure 8.2). We draw our examples of these types from research in Boston and Cambridge, Massachusetts, and across the country. We have chosen to profile these programs because they were particularly suited to distinctions we wished to elaborate.[5]

### Self-Contained programs

Programs that make little or no attempt to collaborate with schools we describe as Self-Contained. These programs usually have such a clearly defined mission that they perceive a stronger connection

**Figure 8.2.   The five types of bridging between schools and after-school programs**

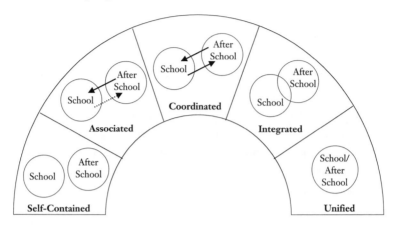

to schools to be potentially threatening, overwhelming, or simply unnecessary. As a result, the youth participants effectively constitute the only connection between school and after-school. While some Self-Contained programs set aside a block of time for homework that students are responsible for using productively, such work is not regarded as the true purpose of the program. The lack of bridging in these programs seems mainly the result of program philosophy rather than location or organizational capacity.

Self-Contained programs tend to fall into two categories: those with strong, self-designed academic curricula and those with a predominating arts, sports, or expeditionary learning focus. Interestingly, we found several programs that aim to promote academic learning despite their lack of connection with the school. These programs view themselves as "second schools"—intensive academic programs of study, delivered in the after-school hours to compensate for the school's failure to reach certain students. These programs generally view the school as dysfunctional or children as requiring more than the school curriculum offers, so they design their methods to counter those of the schools.

One such "second school" program we included in our research. Despite the location of the program in a public school, it is its philosophy to keep bridging to a minimum. Its operating premise is that its "focused, demanding, result-oriented" environment and curriculum propels children to achieve in a way that the standard school curriculum does not.[6] Its focus is for its "scholars" to apply to, be accepted into, and succeed at public exam schools and private schools. The fact that such schools demand more than simply meeting state standards means that the Steppingstone curriculum must go beyond the traditional school curriculum. The program is a rigorous one that requires a fourteen-month commitment from children, and its results are impressive even beyond a selection bias (for example, academic motivation and parental support), with 87 percent of the 2001 scholars getting into exam schools and 90 percent of the 1995 scholars entering college in 2001.

Some Self-Contained programs can compromise their own effectiveness if they become so alienated from the school that they cannot exchange information with teachers and guidance counselors about the overall well-being of children they jointly serve. Even so, it is clear that a great deal of high-quality learning can take place in such programs if the program has well-articulated goals, a curriculum or projects designed to meet those goals, and a staff capable of that kind of learning. Many Self-Contained programs are not project based at all, with a "school outside the school" approach that focuses primarily on skill training. Strong community-based programs often use a project-based approach, but the project reflects the priorities of the programs: productive in relationship to the community but not in terms of academics.

*Associated programs*

Programs that reserve a role for school engagement in their program mission but do not have a strong connection to schools we describe as Associated. We found that a major reason for the lack of connection was that schools or after-school programs have not been responsive to each other's attempts at outreach. Program philosophy and organizational capacity were also influential. The majority of programs we observed or interviewed fell into this category. Community-based programs, in particular, often are found here because of the added challenge that their locations present to bridging efforts.

The specific technique used to make contact with schools differed greatly from program to program but tended to focus on interpersonal bridging. One popular method of outreach was sending surveys or forms to children's teachers that asked for information about academic strengths and weaknesses. Jenny Atkinson, senior director of education and arts for the Boys and Girls Clubs of America, described a form that she used as a staff person at a club. It read: "This child has tutoring once per week. What areas should we focus on to make this time most effective?" Associated programs vary in the persistence with which they try to communicate with school personnel, according to the program's organizational capacity and philosophy. Programs that were more effective in this category achieved increased response rates by combining bridging methods. For example, a program staff person might follow up on written contact with informal contact in the form of the after-school director's introducing herself to the school principal or engaging in some sort of outreach to teachers as well.

Our interviews with programs revealed that Associated programs were limited in the intensity of bridging because the onus tended to fall entirely on the after-school staff. Many schools do not have dedicated teachers of administrators to serve as liaisons with after-school programs. Therefore, the responsibility to bridge falls on programs and on their staff's convincing principals and teachers of the merit of collaborating with them. In many of the community-based YMCA programs, for example, program directors are responsible for bridging, and that responsibility competes with a multitude of other, and usually more pressing, responsibilities that directly and immediately the children. In sum, although there was a basic familiarity between Associated programs and schools, this did not necessarily translate into regular or deep sharing of information or connecting learning in any way other than homework clubs.

In Associated programs, there is some recognition of the academic experiences of children in schools but insufficient knowledge of school content to link after-school programs to academic pursuits. These programs tend to be more focused on tutoring and homework and less on deepening what is being learned during the school day.

### Coordinated programs

Programs that maintain consistent communication and joint learning goals with schools we describe as Coordinated. The difference between a Coordinated and an Associated program is primarily in organizational capacity. Both types share a program philosophy that considers engagement with schools to be an important factor in achieving learning goals. However, Coordinated programs go a step further by dedicating significant staff time—50 percent or more, often at the director level—to create the school connection. These staff efforts allow for more elaborated bridging strategies to be employed, generally including interpersonal and curricular links. We found that there is no consensus yet on the title and training of the person who performs these duties. In a recent report, we have recommended the creating the role of education coordinator in after-school settings.

One highly regarded Boston after-school program can serve as an example of successful interpersonal and curricular bridging realized by an education coordinator. The education coordinator of the school-based program is a presence in the school. With the approval of the principal, she is able to greet teachers informally as she walks through the halls or picks up children at the end of the day. She distributes a brief survey to teachers at the beginning of the year requesting information about the strengths and challenges of children in her program, and she then follows up with teachers in person to discuss specific children. Due to her relationship with teachers, the return rate of the forms is as high as 90 percent. She uses this information on individual children to guide the work of college volunteer tutors whom she supervises and to inform her decisions when purchasing games and educational supplements for the program. She also has access to the children's grades used for an informational and evaluative tool.

Another significant provider of middle school after-school programming in Boston has two curricular approaches to bridging. One is the program's innovative apprenticeship model that brings together disadvantaged adolescents and local professionals to complete a project. Past apprenticeships have ranged from performing a mock trial at a city courthouse facilitated by lawyers and a judge to creating a cookbook with a chef. Academic competencies are taught as they relate to completing the project. In addition, the organization implements a literacy curriculum at all of its sites that is aligned with the standards of the school system.

A common challenge that Coordinated programs face is that although there exists a fairly intense desire to support the school curriculum, the two institutions of after-school and school remain separate. They have an interface through the designated liaison or a part of the after-school curriculum that is aligned with state standards. Nonetheless, the majority of the staff members at the program are uninvolved directly with bridging efforts. This is not necessarily a disadvantage because it does free most staff from the considerable effort required to work with schools. At the same time, the lack of involvement affects the degree to which staff members can fully reinforce or complement school day learning.

Coordinated programs often have a mission that makes projects with a strong skill orientation and even academic content desirable. There is a recognition of children's learning during the school day and beyond. Apprenticeship programs with volunteer experts are a good example. Projects are professionalized, and leadership is usually handed over to nonteachers, but they have a strong educational focus. They are not as oriented toward youth participation as projects often are in free-standing and associated programs. Instead, they tend to be focused on expert knowledge. This approach helps address one hurdle of after-school education: that many staff are overwhelmed by the complexity of project-based learning.

### Integrated programs

Programs that engage in a systemic or institutional relationship with schools we describe as Integrated. At this intensity of bridging, both the program and the school have identified the other as an important partner in achieving their learning and developmental goals. In addition, the after-school program develops an organizational structure that will allow it to devote staff time and resources to interpersonal, curricular, and systemic bridging, and these are reciprocal investments on the part of the school. Here, the after-school program and school share space, staff, and procedures. Clear curricular continuities exist. An after-school director may obtain a grant for equipment, such as computers, that directly benefits the day program, or the two institutions may apply for grants collaboratively. Administrative structures support shared goal setting and the easy flow of information back and forth. Two important indicators that a program is Integrated are that the after-school director is part of the school leadership team and that school personnel are on the program's advisory board.

An in-school/after-school academic and mental health intervention at a number of middle schools in Boston, Cleveland, and San Francisco, developed by faculty at Harvard University, exemplifies the integrated bridging type. The program has developed a new professional role called *prevention practitioners*: youth development specialists who bring together knowledge of education, community development, and mental health practices. Practitioners work in classrooms two days per week while they are in session, providing academic and behavioral support to the whole class and extra services to children identified as particularly at risk. Practitioners also staff their own after-school programs for students they work with during the day, which reinforces the program's focus on academic and mental health resiliency, through different methods. Teachers also participate in the after-school program. The classroom and after-school programs require close collaboration between teachers and practitioners. The program is part of the school support and leadership teams. This integrated approach provides continuities for the "whole" child as well on other children in the classroom and yields many benefits for learning.

In Integrated programs, projects can become very school focused. Because youth workers or extended-day teachers also work in classrooms, classroom activities can be meaningfully connected to after-school learning. This can lead to projects that enrich school-day learning without becoming school. The link can be not only through curricula but also through people who are familiar with the school's learning goals. This can lead to projects that enrich school-day learning through exploration and hands-on activities and even the development of joint projects between schools and after-school programs.

### Unified programs

Unified programs are almost indistinguishable from school because they are on-site and are part of a truly extended school day. The extended day in this intensity of bridging does not mean that school has wholly infiltrated the after-school program. Instead, the day incorporates the best of both worlds and weaves them together seamlessly. There are very few programs that truly fit this description.[7] However, there are some private schools that aspire to this goal. The full-service school models introduced in other chapters of this volume can also fall into this category.

The vision for the potential of such programs is strong. De Kanter, Huff, and Chung contend that a model we call Unified would enable schools to address subjects that have been increasingly viewed as supplemental or peripheral to schools' academic goals.[8] At the Unified level, there are no projects that happen solely during the school day or the after-school program. Projects tend to permeate the entire educational experience of the child. It remains to be seen whether this vision can be realized in public schools, whether it will be successful in cross-pollinating the purposes and methods of school and after-school, and what practices in particular are most effective.

### Summary of bridging typology

The typology we have provided describes the great diversity in means and ends of bridging between after-school programs and schools. This discussion is important for schools, funders, and parents, but we see a particular relevance for after-school providers who can use the typology to identify themselves within the spectrum and determine whether they are bridging in a way that is consonant with their own program goals. Each type has slightly different characteristics, such as the difference in organizational capacity between Coordinated and Associated programs or the increased institutional bridging among Integrated and Unified programs. Program directors who want to effect change should use these salient features as cues when thinking about how to move from one category to another.[9]

## Conclusion

We found that some essential bridging is already occurring in most programs, homework clubs, and homework help. We call this type of learning "extended" because it is entirely dominated by the school, usually involuntary, because teachers demand it of children, and parents want it done before they return home. Homework is a form of learning that usually provides little room for program staff or youth to act independently and creatively. Few people argue with this form of bridging, but we need to expand our notions of bridging considerably. After-school time should not be just more school; it should provide children and youth with a different space and experience.

It is not the location of a program that will define or predetermine bridging efforts. Some programs that are located in school remain very hostile or indifferent to the school day, while other programs that are free-standing are engaged with the content of school learning and view their mission as supporting children's academic success. Many productive and creative forms of bridging are springing up all over the country. Some of the best ones are embracing some of the curricular goals of the school day, including science, language, and social studies, and building community-focused and enriching projects that invite youth participation. The Museum of Natural History example provides an excellent model. It also demonstrates the potential usefulness of bridging. The children chose a topic that connected them to their families, a collective working out of illness and loss, that had strong parental support. The effort also required school resources, a school audience to raise the money, and a staff that was knowledgeable about the writing, conceptual, and math abilities the children brought to their task.

Many programs proudly proclaim that they are achieving academic success in their projects. But analysis of the academic component shows that it is very marginal. A cooking class should not be viewed primarily as a math class. Although measurement is involved, academic learning does take some level of explicit skill training. It is perfectly fine for children to cook and enjoy the success of learning these skills. Programs should not count only if they are tied to academic outcomes. Indeed, translating and evaluating every activity in terms of academic outcomes is a sign of too much bridging, a form of giving in to principles that take away from the identity and goals of after-school programs. But if certain tasks, like subtracting and adding, are connected to the curriculum of the school day, as they were in the Cancer Society project, and the skills are honed and practiced, significant gains result. What is more, these outcomes will be enhanced by the children's motivation to learn them in order to perform the exciting project tasks.

Because after-school projects are labor intensive, expensive, and time-consuming, making connections to the learning of the school day and being able to access resources of the school day can be very productive. What we have to avoid is having the children and staff experience the projects just as more school instead of as a creative extension of learning that is more hands on, more participatory, and more community focused. And even these kinds of learning activities and projects should not take up the entire after-school time; there should be time for play, recreation, and the arts. Furthermore, extended and enriched learning can be considered an alternative to homework help because it serves, among other things, as a creative form of deepening of classroom learning. And finally, such an endeavor has the potential to produce a two-way bridge, running from the after school to the school as well.

Linking different learning approaches to secure success for children can lead to join professional training, joint planning, and even integrated administration of certain programs. Certainly, there are dangers, especially if this effort becomes a pretext on the part of schools and school districts to control the budgets of after-school programs. But a vision of increased bridging implies connecting different identities between schools, families, and after-schools. It should make us committed to develop strategies that benefit all organizations involved, most importantly the children and families served. How else would we get the children of the American Cancer Society project to learn academic content, produce art, and learn how to buy and sell and budget, and all while generously donating money on behalf of themselves and their families to a major organization fighting illness? Is that not what learning is ultimately about for all parties involved? Certainly it is if our goal is to produce environments where we combine learning with responsibility and excitement.

## Notes

1. Noam, G., Biancarosa, G., & Dechausay, N. (2002). *Learning beyond school: Developing the field of after-school education.* Cambridge, MA: Program in Afterschool Education and Research.

2. Noam, G. (2001, May 10–11). *After-school time: Toward a theory of collaboration.* Paper presented at the Urban Seminar Series on Children's Mental Health and Safety: Out of School Time, Kennedy School of Government, Cambridge, MA.

3. Noam, G., Winner, K., Rhein, A., & Molad, B. (1996). The Harvard RALLY program and the prevention practitioner: Comprehensive, school-based intervention to support resiliency in at-risk adolescents. *Journal of Child and Youth Care Work, 11,* 32–47.

4. Noam (2001); Noam, G., Pucci, K., & Foster, E. (1999). Development, resilience, and school success in youth: The prevention practitioner and the Harvard-RALLY program. In D. Cicchetti & S. Toth (Eds.), *Developmental approaches to prevention and intervention.* Rochester, NY: University of Rochester Press.

5. It is important to note that some of the profiled programs—including the YMCA, Boys and Girls Club, B.E.L.L. Foundation, and Citizen Schools—are one of multiple sites. In these cases, we can speak with authority only about the site where we interviewed.

6. Blythe, T., Wilson, D., Noam, G., Boyd, J., Griffin, P., & Greenebaum, S. (2003). *Fun learning matters.* Cambridge, MA: Harvard University and the Afterschool Corporation.

7. Although one of Boston Excels' primary objectives is to ensure "that all school partnerships contribute to school goals," thereby potentially promoting high alignment between school and after school, this alignment does not

reach the unified level of intensity because this level is characterized by an extended school day for all students and by school and after school essentially being indistinguishable from one another.

8. De Kanter, A., Huff, M., & Chung, A. M. (2002, May 17–18). *Supplementation vs. supplantation: What is the core of schooling and what is supplemental?* Paper presented at the Afterschool Programs and Supplementary Education Conference, New York.

9. For further discussion, see Caplan, J., & Calfee, C. S. (2000). *Strengthening connections between schools and after-school programs.* Naperville, IL: North Central Regional Educational Laboratory. Available on-line: http://www.ncrel.org/21stcclc/connect/index.html.

GIL G. NOAM *is a clinical and developmental psychologist at Harvard University and McLean Hospital and with his team creates learning communities and prevention programs in school and after-school settings.*

# Index

# Back Issue/Subscription Order Form

Copy or detach and send to:
**Jossey-Bass, A Wiley Company, 989 Market Street, San Francisco CA 94103-1741**

**Call or fax toll-free: Phone 888-378-2537; Fax 888-481-2665**

Back Issues:     Please send me the following issues at $28 each
(Important: please include issue ISBN)

_____

_____

$ _____     Total for single issues

$ _____     SHIPPING CHARGES:  SURFACE     Domestic Canadian
                                    First Item    $5.00      $6.00
                                    Each Add'l Item  $3.00    $1.50
                 Please call for next day, second day, or international shipping rates.

Subscriptions    Please ❏ start ❏ renew my subscription to *New Directions for Youth Development* at the following rate:

|   |   |   |
|---|---|---|
| U.S. | ❏ Individual $75 | ❏ Institutional $149 |
| Canada | ❏ Individual $75 | ❏ Institutional $189 |
| All Others | ❏ Individual $99 | ❏ Institutional $223 |
| Online Subscription | | ❏ Institutional $149 |

**For more information about online subscriptions visit
www.interscience.wiley.com**

-- _____     Are you eligible for our **Student Subscription Rate**? Attach a copy of your current Student Identification Card and deduct 20% from the regular subscription rate.

$ _____     Total single issues and subscriptions (Add appropriate sales tax for your state for single issue orders. No sales tax for U.S. subscriptions. Canadian residents, add GST for subscriptions and single issues.)

❏Payment enclosed (U.S. check or money order only)
❏VISA ❏ MC ❏ AmEx ❏ Discover Card #_____ Exp. Date _____
               Your credit card payment will be charged to John Wiley & Sons.

Signature _____ Day Phone _____
❏ Bill Me (U.S. institutional orders only. Purchase order required.)

Purchase order # _____
               Federal Tax ID13559302                    GST 89102 8052

Name _____

Address _____

_____

Phone _____ E-mail _____

**PROMOTION CODE ND3**

# Other Titles Available

NEW DIRECTIONS FOR YOUTH DEVELOPMENT: THEORY, PRACTICE, AND RESEARCH
Gil G. Noam, Editor-in-Chief

YD96    **Youth Participation: Improving Institutions and Communities**
*Benjamin Kirshner, Jennifer L. O'Donoghue, Milbrey McLaughlin*
Explores the growing effort in youth organizations, community development, and schools and other public institutions to foster meaningful activities that empower adolescents to participate in decision making that affects their lives and to take action on issues they care about. Pushing against long-held, culturally specific ideas about adolescence as well as institutional barriers to youth involvement, the efforts of these organizations engaged in youth participation programs deserve careful analysis and support. This volume offers an assessment of the field, as well as specific chapters that chronicle efforts to achieve youth participation across a variety of settings and dimensions.
*ISBN 0-7879-6339-9*

YD95    **Pathways to Positive Development Among Diverse Youth**
*Richard M. Lerner, Carl S. Taylor, Alexander von Eye*
Positive youth development represents an emerging emphasis in developmental thinking that is focused on the incredible potential of adolescents to maintain healthy trajectories and develop resilience, even in the face of myriad negative influences. This volume discusses the theory, research, policy, and programs that take this strength-based, positive development approach to diverse youth. Examines theoretical ideas about the nature of positive youth development, and about the related concepts of thriving and well-being, as well as current and needed policy strategies, "best practice" in youth-serving programs, and promising community-based efforts to marshal the developmental assets of individuals and communities to enhance thriving among youth.
*ISBN 0-7879-6338-0*

YD94    **Youth Development and After-School Time: A Tale of Many Cities**
*Gil G. Noam, Beth Miller*
This issue looks at exciting citywide and cross-city initiatives in after-school time. It presents case studies of youth-related work that combines large-scale policy, developmental thinking, innovative programming, as well as research and evaluation. Chapters discuss efforts of community-based organizations, museums, universities,

schools, and clinics who are joining forces, sharing funding and other resources and jointly creating a system of after-school care and education.
*ISBN 0-7879-6337-2*

YD93    **A Critical View of Youth Mentoring**
*Jean E. Rhodes*
Mentoring has become an almost essential aspect of youth development and is expanding beyond the traditional one-to-one, volunteer, community-based mentoring. This volume provides evidence of the benefits of enduring high-quality mentoring programs, as well as apprenticeships, advisories, and other relationship-based programs that show considerable promise. Authors examine mentoring in the workplace, teacher-student interaction, and the mentoring potential of student advising programs. They also take a critical look at the importance of youth-adult relationships and how a deeper understanding of these relationships can benefit youth mentoring. This issue raises important questions about relationship-based interventions and generates new perspectives on the role of adults in the lives of youth.
*ISBN 0-7879-6294-5*

YD92    **Zero Tolerance: Can Suspension and Expulsion Keep Schools Safe?**
*Russell J. Skiba, Gil G. Noam*
Addressing the problem of school violence and disruption requires thoughtful understanding of the complexity of the personal and systemic factors that increase the probability of violence, and designing interventions based on that understanding. This inaugural issue explores the effectiveness of zero tolerance as a tool for promoting school safety and improving student behavior and offer alternative strategies that work.
*ISBN 0-7879-1441-X*

# NEW DIRECTIONS FOR YOUTH DEVELOPMENT
# IS NOW AVAILABLE ONLINE AT WILEY INTERSCIENCE

## What is Wiley InterScience?

*Wiley InterScience* is the dynamic online content service from John Wiley & Sons delivering the full text of over 300 leading scientific, technical, medical, and professional journals, plus major reference works, the acclaimed *Current Protocols* laboratory manuals, and even the full text of select Wiley print books online.

## What are some special features of Wiley InterScience?

*Wiley InterScience Alerts* is a service that delivers table of contents via e-mail for any journal available on Wiley InterScience as soon as a new issue is published online.
*Early View* is Wiley's exclusive service presenting individual articles online as soon as they are ready, even before the release of the compiled print issue. These articles are complete, peer-reviewed, and citable.
*CrossRef* is the innovative multi-publisher reference linking system enabling readers to move seamlessly from a reference in a journal article to the cited publication, typically located on a different server and published by a different publisher.

## How can I access Wiley InterScience?

Visit http://www.interscience.wiley.com

*Guest Users* can browse Wiley InterScience for unrestricted access to journal Tables of Contents and Article Abstracts, or use the powerful search engine.
*Registered Users* are provided with a *Personal Home Page* to store and manage customized alerts, searches, and links to favorite journals and articles. Additionally, Registered Users can view free Online Sample Issues and preview selected material from major reference works.
*Licensed Customers* are entitled to access full-text journal articles in PDF, with select journals also offering full-text HTML.

## How do I become an Authorized User?

*Authorized Users* are individuals authorized by a paying Customer to have access to the journals in Wiley InterScience. For example, a university that subscribes to Wiley journals is considered to be the Customer. Faculty, staff and students authorized by the university to have access to those journals in Wiley InterScience are Authorized Users. Users should contact their Library for information on which Wiley journals they have access to in Wiley InterScience.

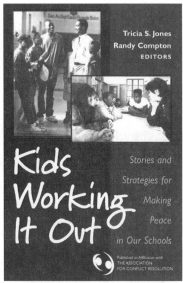